CHRIS MADDEN
THE SOUL OF A HOUSE

Decorating with Warmth,
Style, and Comfort

THE SOUL OF A HOUSE

Decorating with Warmth, Style, and Comfort

RIZZOLI
NEW YORK

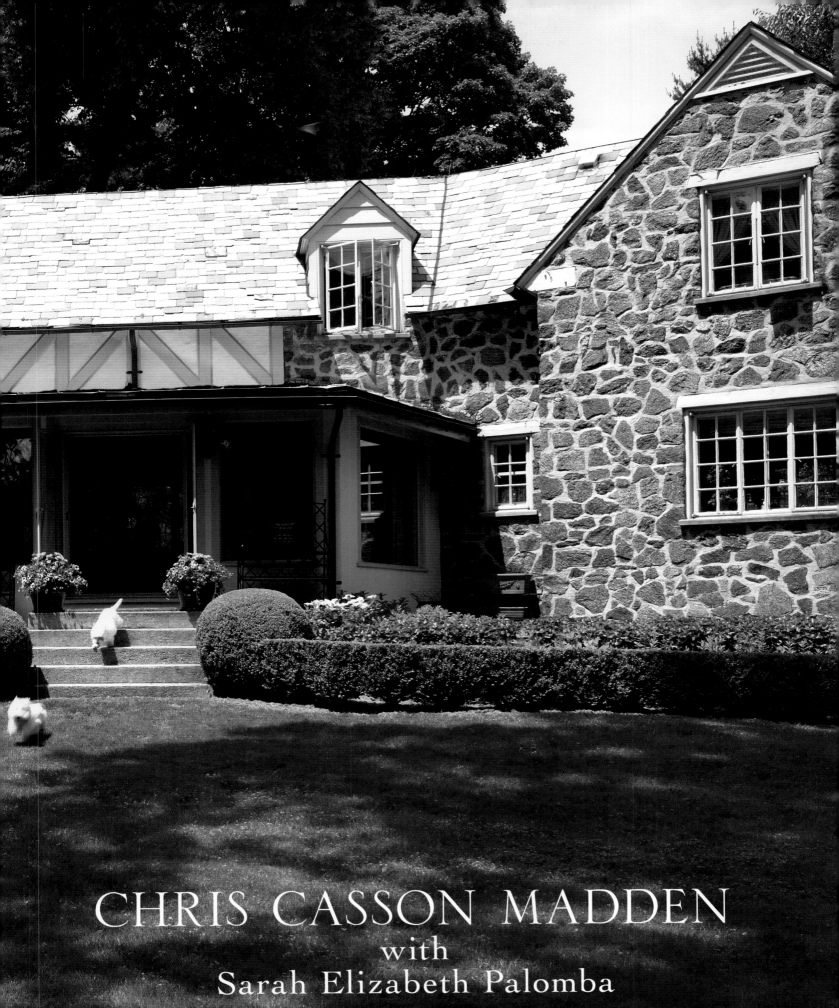

CHRIS CASSON MADDEN
with
Sarah Elizabeth Palomba

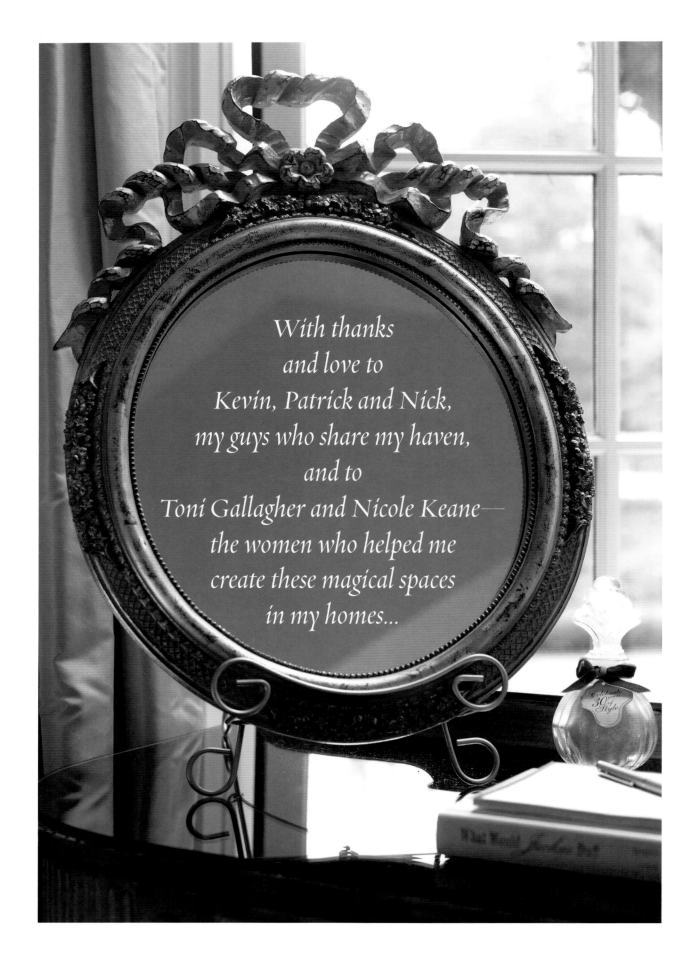

With thanks
and love to
Kevin, Patrick and Nick,
my guys who share my haven,
and to
Toni Gallagher and Nicole Keane—
the women who helped me
create these magical spaces
in my homes...

CONTENTS

OPPOSITE, CLOCKWISE FROM UPPER LEFT: *One of my favorite pastimes, cutting flowers from the garden before guests arrive; a creamware tea set; these found apothecary jars were used to keep specimens for scientific work in Africa; a bouquet of fresh sunflowers from my garden.*

INTRODUCTION

I'm a lover of houses. I peruse real estate brochures like fashionistas read *Vogue* and *Bazaar* and, on Sundays, go straight to the back of the real estate section in the *New York Times Magazine* to fantasize about the intriguing "for sale" listings. I've always had a special interest in "orphan homes": what I like to call that unique genre of houses—some aging, some neglected—that have been on the market a tad too long and earned unjust reputations as "stale," "white elephants," or, perhaps, a bit beyond their prime.

Those white elephants—whether contemporary architecture or traditional—always call out to me in some inexplicable way, whether I've had the opportunity to photograph one for my many design books or explore another, with a friend tagging along.

Over the years, my husband, Kevin, and I have bought several of those unique places, dating from our first purchase of literally one of the smallest cottages in East Hampton on Long Island in New York, many years ago, to our first real "grown-up house" in Rye, New York, which had been on the market for three years and where we raised our two sons, to our present home—a rambling early-twentieth-century carriage house, which had lingered on the market for several years—to our mid-century-modern little getaway in southern Vermont (rescued by us after almost five years on the shelf).

The aesthetic and architectural qualities of a house's interior spaces, and obviously its setting, are what initially pique my interest, but what really intrigues me is what I like to call the "soul" of a house— that sometimes ephemeral and often indescribable yet tantalizing quality that I (and I know I'm not alone in this) instantly can sense when I'm stepping into a home, be it large or small.

It has been my great good fortune to have chosen a career path that has enabled me to cross the thresholds of hundreds of residences. And what I have learned from these places is that the aura of soul is often a combination of the skilled craft of an architect or designer along with, in most instances, the inspired work of the homeowners, who imbue their space with a distinct personality that gives it a feeling of warmth, comfort, and their own unique inspiration, passion, and memories. Soul is an attribute—an intangible one that rises above price tags and neighborhoods—and it demands not just an understanding of a place's "bones" but also the ability to incorporate one's personal vision into its decoration.

I know when we first walked into our century-old carriage house I felt an immediate sense of "coming home." It had the charming feel of an old French farmhouse—even in the rooms that were stripped bare of furniture and painted a shiny, clear white.

Yet the hallmark of any special place with true soul is that, regardless of its pedigree, it always seems to brim with the personal signature and memories of its inhabitants—reflected perhaps in an entrance hall lined with framed antique maps that have been collected over the years, a bookcase-lined wall in an unexpected place, a gently worn paisley throw discovered at a yard sale, or an array of well-used copper pots hanging in a kitchen window.

I am often asked how one respects the sensibility of a place while transforming it into one's own haven—a design philosophy that I first espoused in earnest in the early 1990s, a period of enormous technological change in this country as computers, cell phones, fax machines, etc., altered the landscape in almost every aspect of our lives. I have found the secret to creating a personal haven while maintaining the architectural integrity of one's home lies in understanding how to layer items both old and new, practical and personal, to create a cohesive aesthetic. And that philosophy of haven is a tenet that continues to be one of my main decorating beliefs to this day.

A good friend of mine (and former head of Chanel) described years ago that at the end of a "show"—in fashion terms—he would notice that the models leaving the back doors of the French fashion houses were wearing blue jeans paired with couture jackets (usually from that season). Today, I frequently see that same élan for mixing up old and new in those dwellings that I love to visit over and over again. By combining some newly acquired treasure with a historic or vintage one, a layering of the old and the new is created, contributing to a home's sense of soul—making it more than simply a repository of objects.

Another aspect of creating soul that I've tried to achieve in my own home is what I refer to as the six senses, which help to evoke, as Proust or Dickens might say, a remembrance of things past—and perhaps to come. The sixth sense of emotional connectedness can sometimes be as simple as a child's small handprint pressed into a ceramic circle, or a favorite book that instantly takes one back to the moment when a memory was created.

The other five senses—sight, scent, sound, touch, and taste—can easily be incorporated into every room in one's home. It can be as simple as a bathroom filled with a fresh pitcher of water and slices of fruit; a view out a window (or a great photograph or painting); music chimes or a small fountain with its melodious drip; the softness of a pile of fresh towels; or the aroma of lavender and eucalyptus oils (or the scent of your favorite candle)—all these can change your emotional well-being for the better as you enter that particular room.

And as you journey through my family's home in New York and our special getaway in Vermont, I hope you'll discover how I've experimented with, and enjoyed, incorporating *objets* and gems that have been a part of my—and my family's—life, whether it's a simple rock found on the beaches of Long Island decades ago, framed menus from memorable gatherings at favorite restaurants, or an assemblage of porcelain dogs collected over the years—their commonality is that they all simply say "home."

GRACE   HOWELL CONANT

AT HOME

OPPOSITE: *A collage of the three generations of the men in my life on a vintage glass and wooden tray.*

Circa 1916

Carriage houses are the epitome of romance, whether real or imagined. They bring together all of the elements of some of my most favorite and timeless essentials: horses, automobiles, and idiosyncratic layouts with stone edifices, filled with an abundance of architectural details. Often a gathering spot for "ladies and gentlemen" awaiting their cars and carriages, they were originally introduced during the colonial era in this country and were strictly utilitarian. They were built not just to accommodate horses, but also their hay and accoutrements and, of course, to house the stable boys and footmen above.

Because of their high ceilings and ingenious layouts, carriage houses inspire and intrigue. They have acquired an aura of panache and cachet that makes them extremely appealing to so many—from young couples on bucolic suburban estates to urban contemporary artists. So when a carriage house came up for sale in our adjacent town, I was first intrigued by the unique dwelling and then entranced, which began my love affair—along with its challenges and foibles—with the home we live in today.

Its location was the next seductive piece of the puzzle. It backed up to the property where one of my heroines, Amelia Earhart, an early adventurer and feminist, often took her small plane with its fold-up wings, out to nearby fields—via a car—taking off and landing for an afternoon spin before heading back to the home that she shared with publisher George P. Putnam on what is now called Amelia Earhart Lane in Rye, New York.

The original manor house (a thirty-six-room English Tudor mansion, since torn down), along with the gatekeeper lodge and gatehouse and our present carriage house, was a collaboration between a wealthy philanthropist, George Arents Jr., founder of the American Machine and Foundry Company, and Louis Colt Albro, a noted architect from New York City who studied under Stanford White.

Circa 2010

As the *New York Times* real estate page noted in November of 1915, Arents paid "$125,000 for the Westchester acreage, which consisted of 2 parcels of land (25 acres in a triangular slice and the other being an adjoining 54 acres for an additional $125,000)." Arents, according to the *Times* article, contemplated "turning the property into an English Park." The project was completed in 1916, and as the prestigious *Architectural Record* reported in April of 1918 in a lengthy article about the completed project, "Hillbrook [the manor house] . . . stands well back on the site, permitting a view over the owner's land. The entrance to it is through a long driveway . . ." This is most likely where our carriage house stands today and, although close to a major thoroughfare, our carriage house revealed some of its early history when, digging around with one of my sons, we discovered a road under a moss-covered path that led directly from the stable section of our carriage house—now our enclosed dining room—to the present-day parkway below our hills.

Although there isn't any mention in the historical records of the "remise," as carriage houses were sometimes called, I often wonder if—almost one hundred years later—its original owners and architect knew that their work would blossom with its enchanting aspects and cozy ambiance to entice our family into—after just one look—buying the home that we would want to spend our days and nights in.

Our carriage house and part of the manor house were situated to have views of the meadows and brooks on the estate, making the most of the flat landscape of southern Westchester County. Yet, the *Architectural Record* also noted in a review of the completed property that the "south front needs the effects of time and of vines to soften the 'quoins' [the cornerstones of brick or stone walls] concealing them here and there or else softening their angles with tiny spots and shadows. All this much needed harmony will come in the course of years when the full effect of planting is apparent." And so it has.

As the future owners of one of the more humble dwellings on the Hillbrook estate, we were fortunate to be the beneficiaries of the long-ago owners' strategies and landscaping philosophies, and today, its rolling lawns, towering oak, maple, and dogwood trees, along with cherry and apple-blossom arbors, are balanced by slate terraces and vine-covered stone walls adorned with artful architectural details.

We continued the original owners' vision of an "English Park" with the addition of more plantings and gardens—including annuals and perennials, bird feeders and birdbaths—throughout the grounds.

Inspired by the late Gertrude Jekyll, a noted garden designer, I placed benches and garden stools around the property to take full advantage of the walls and gardens. Jekyll effectively accomplished this in her many landscaping projects over the last century and, as she wrote, "it is not the paint that makes the picture, but the brain and heart and hand of the man who uses it."

PREVIOUS SPREAD: *The entry to the carriage house, which is adjoined to a seamless addition on its left, utilizing the same local quarry stone.*
ABOVE: *The enclosed stable and carriage area as seen from the driveway.*
OPPOSITE: *Waxed-paper parasols in flowering urns are a welcome note of whimsy to the pastel impatiens alongside the walkway with a glimpse of the gardens beyond.*

CLOCKWISE FROM UPPER LEFT: *Antique and new architectural details abound—vintage and electrical lanterns light each entryway; a resin architectural element of my design; a piece of the original manor house becomes a garden sculpture; a stone lion's head; a young reader amidst the garden of ivy; a lion's-head fountain on the back terrace; a French fleur-de-lys beveled-glass insert in an original antique oak door; a timeless sundial catches the sun's rays.* CENTER: *The fleur-de-lys crest above the garage.*

18

PART I

HOME FIRES

MONIA MACROCOSMICA   TASCHEN

WELCOME HOME

The entryway is usually the first impression that friends, guests, and family get of one's home. Yet we were presented with a conundrum since our house had three front entryways. This unusual layout was the work of a savvy previous homeowner who, looking to add on to the carriage house's original footprint, was able to locate the same exterior stone used in the home's construction in a quarry nearby and, with the help of some creative reconfiguring and talented stonemasons, designed a seamless addition, providing the house with not only more living space but also those numerous entryways! We were faced with the challenge of creating three separate looks for our thresholds, which was a job I took pleasure in, once I decided upon each one's design direction.

One entrance leads to the more formal rooms, and I decided to take a cue from my sister Jeanne's home in Paris, where she covered and lacquered the walls in a small room with the lovely typeface of newspapers from Asia. At an auction held at the Equinox Hotel in southern Vermont, I once bid on boxes of antique books—not sure what treasures would be in each. Some were extraordinary delights—*Houses and Gardens*, by Sir Edwin Lutyen, R.A., Gertrude Jekyll's *Wood and Garden*, and at the very bottom of the container, a threadbare collection of Boston Architectural Club yearbooks from the '20s. With the help of two talented artisans, I decoupaged our small eight-walled, forty-five-square-foot entry to our living and dining rooms with some of those dog-eared but enchanting pages from the club's yearbooks, which contained remarkable examples of English architecture and ornament—quite fitting, I think, for our home and its romantic history.

An antique mirror with

PREVIOUS SPREAD: *An oversized Mayan head fills a clean-lined window and fresh pineapples on either side provide a hint of scent as well as a symbol of welcome. A collection of books also helps to set the tone.* ABOVE: *How I usually greet our guests—a dog in my arms and sometimes one or two following behind—all saying, "Welcome."* OPPOSITE: *A gargoyle-framed mirror is central to this tiny hallway whose walls are covered with decoupaged pages. A custom-crafted radiator cover is in the corner. The oak door's glass fleur-de-lys insert is glimpsed in the mirror.*

a gargoyle motif, which has traveled with me from early apartments and various houses to this home, hangs above a uniquely covered radiator—one of two heating units that took some creative reworking to help them blend into such a small space.

Many years ago, I transformed a pair of antique Venetian gilt candlesticks with a similar gargoyle motif into handsome lamps that give off a lovely ambient light when guests are arriving—a time when I'll usually dim the more practical high-hat lighting overhead.

On my annual visit to the Philadelphia Flower Show, I fell in love with five stone mushrooms created by a talented artist from Wales, who—inspired by mushrooms he found in the Celtic countryside—created each one individually in cement. I placed

them in a weather-beaten container, secured them with green Oasis floral foam, and covered the foam with moss. Their weight and tilting adds, I think, to their authenticity and beauty.

Since I always try to bring all five senses into each room of our home, before guests are due to arrive I like to insert two fresh pineapples from the market into our carved wood plant containers to add

a bit of sight, scent, touch, and, eventually, taste.

The second entry, located in the center of the house, leads into our wine room, known to all as my husband's "oenophile's delight" (and a room our friends often gravitate to). It is clearly and primarily a room with all the accoutrements that go with that genre, but it's also a charming and unexpected entrance to our home.

Our third entryway, adjacent to the driveway and garage, is the one my family uses much of the time. I can usually tell by the number of my sons' and husband's shoes that collect in that space—which led me to create a "home" for those sizes 10, 11, and 12 running shoes and galoshes. An oversized grapevine basket, complete with a woven top, is where my guys know to dig when a shoe or boot is missing.

To transform it into a smaller, cozier entryway and a practical place to drop hats, keys, gloves, and dog leashes, an arched wall was added to separate this foyer from our family room, and it was painted a deep brown—inspired by the late, legendary designer Mark Hampton and his iconic room at the Kips Bay Showhouse many years ago.

ABOVE: *A quill pen and ink, found during a visit to Paris, catch the summer light.*
OPPOSITE: *The prologue to our home: walking sticks and umbrellas rest in the foreground, a uniquely reconfigured French antique table covers the radiator, while guests are fascinated by the myriad blueprints decoupaged as "wallpaper" on our entry walls.*

CELEBRATIONS

hether dining with friends by the glow of candlelight or enjoying a sun-filled late-morning brunch while listening to the music of Cole Porter, Steve Tyrell, or Bebel Gilberto, it's difficult for me to grasp that almost a century ago our generously sized dining room, flanked by its massive thirteen-inch-thick stone pillars and walls with floor-to-ceiling windows, was occupied by a Ford Model T and exposed, so I've been told, to the wind, rain, snow, and heat of the four seasons on both ends. Today, with its transformation from carriage house to versatile space that serves splendidly as a dining room, sun room, and reading room, it resonates with an indelible reminder of its pedigree while, at the same time, reveling in its newfound roles.

When I first walked through this room, accompanied by my family on a late-fall afternoon, I was thrilled at the design possibilities that lay ahead, but also filled with some trepidation about how to imbue this room with a sense of today's comfort and practicality.

I wanted to maintain the architectural feel of a room in which automobiles and horses were once tended to and also to keep the dramatic background of the arched wooden ceiling that gives the room its strong foundation.

I chose the grayish-white color of the grout used in the stone walls as my paint color to enhance the room's appealing sensibility. Slipcovers in that same off-white tone, made from a sturdy cotton duck and monogrammed—a designer trick I've used for over two decades to elevate plain napkins, slipcovers, and bed linens—help lighten the room in the spring and summer while softening the coldness of the stone.

I also gradually began to grasp the previous homeowners' process of transforming this room—their clever addition of the leaded-glass mullioned windows and the handsome French doors across the room, which maintained its architectural integrity while letting us feel warm and snug in

ABOVE: *A corner of the carriage house thoroughfare.*
OPPOSITE: *A collection of some of my favorite things combined with natural objects and old oyster shells used as place cards.*

RIGHT: *Everything is balanced by the cream-and-taupe-hued tones of our dining room— from the natural tabletop elements to the oversized candles and candlesticks that reflect the green beauty of the gardens and lawns beyond.*

ABOVE: *The leaded windows, added to this room when it was enclosed, provide a bird's-eye view of our outside window box while creating a shelf for my indoor plants.*
OPPOSITE: *The ideal setting—a cool room with dappled light and a glass-topped, two-tiered table for some of my ivy topiaries and a few of my favorite orchid plants (there are over thirty-five thousand species), while a gift from my brother Paul and sister-in-law Liz, a wooden figure from the American Folk Art Museum in New York City, surveys all.*

the winter months and cool and breezy in the warmer spring and summer days.

An added attraction for me was that the French doors open to the steps that lead down to our herb and flower gardens, which I planted for cooking and cutting, and they also afford easy access to our awning-covered terrace—an outdoor gathering spot for weekend breakfasts and coffee, backyard grilling, and after-dinner drinks in the evening—weather permitting, of course!

And since I am an avid amateur gardener year-round, my pair of rectangular glass and iron caster plant stands help maintain that sun room feel in the

colder months with their mixtures of ferns, miniature lemon trees, rose bushes, and beloved species of orchids, while my favorite horticulture books, collected over the years, fit perfectly underneath.

Because it's a room for bringing friends and family together, I wanted to make it as inviting as possible by creating a complete opposite axis of separation than its original plan permitted, simply by changing its layout from a walk-through space into one with two dining areas. On one side of the room, a sofa, two open cupboards, and a pair of comfortable chairs are pulled up to a circular table—a perfect setting for Kevin and me to enjoy a quiet breakfast or intimate dinner.

Opposite is one long mahogany table that seats eight with views of the gardens in the summer and snowy evenings in the winter, when the true celebratory spirit of our dining room—filled with our loved ones—flourishes. At those times, nothing makes me more content in this decidedly unique gem of a room than when the work of planning menus, creating table settings and seating arrangements, and cooking is over and everyone lingers long afterward at our dining table with the magic of lively conversation—a poignant reminder to me of the oak table around which my eight brothers and sisters and I grew up, telling stories, news of the day, and secrets that only siblings can share.

ABOVE: Personal and practical, monograms and slipcovers—two of my oft-used design elements, discovered many decades ago—still remain a constant in much of my decorating schemes to this day. OPPOSITE: To invite guests to sit a bit longer at our dining table, I always have comfortable seating, such as this white linen and wood settee, which works perfectly against the room's stone walls alongside a West Indian–style table of my design.

PREVIOUS SPREAD: *An overview of the dining area of our carriage house: Here is where the horses, buggies, carriages, and early automobiles were readied for guests and owners alike. Although now enclosed, the original ceiling created an overarching curve above.*
ABOVE AND OPPOSITE: *Ferns can often soften strong lines of furniture, as this one does atop a pastiche of objects gathered from both my garden and around the world and nestled here into one of my early furniture designs.*

DINING STORAGE

While each family has its own personal traditions and customs with regard to gathering around the table to "break bread," there are certain general guidelines that can make the experience a bit easier and allow the hostess and/or chef to enjoy the fruits of his or her labor. Over the years I've learned that organization is one of the primary keys to this room. Here are some of the tips that I use to keep my dining room both functional and aesthetically pleasing:

■ Work your tabletop accessories into your décor: Assorted items, such as plates, pitchers, and napkin rings, are not only fun to collect but can also be a reflection of your personal style as well. I'm an avid collector of tableware and *objets* and am known among friends for unexpected and often amusing table settings and centerpieces, such as sand from our local beach with starfish and shells interspersed, or piles of pinto beans set with small framed photos of my guests. I like to keep my collection of white pitchers on open shelves in my dining room so it's accessible when needed, but it also adds a decorative element

and picks up the "white" of the walls and ceiling.

■ Group your linens: When preparing for a dinner party, one last-minute stress is when a hostess cannot find a complete set of matching napkins for the table. I'll often mix and match when that happens, but I try to avoid that with a system I devised. I keep all my sets of napkins grouped together with ribbon or string and label each with a little paper tag and a number. Take this process one step further and you can organize your sets by color so that you can mix or coordinate at a moment's notice.

■ Group your silverware: Following that same strategy, flatware and silverware (and I love to collect odd silver pieces or cutlery at tag sales and flea markets) can also be grouped by set to save time. I separate the spoons, knives, and forks and then tie, number, and label them so that I can pull together whichever works best for my table setting at the drop of a hat—or again, mix and sometimes match!

■ Keep inventories: For each room of my home, I have a binder containing all things pertinent to that particular space, be they appliance manuals, inventory lists, or repairmen's phone numbers. I find this system to be particularly valuable with regard to my dining room. In this room's binder, I catalog past guest lists and invitations, and even photographs of table settings, and keep an inventory of all items stored in the many cabinets and drawers of the room. Having a go-to binder for reference keeps me ahead of the game and helps with unexpected mishaps.

OPPOSITE, CLOCKWISE FROM UPPER LEFT: *My collection of cutlery— contemporary and traditional, inherited and found. Similar pieces are grouped and assigned the same numbers; creamware and country-white pitchers—perfect for drinks, flowers, or just display; I began collecting my ever-expanding assortment of napkins on a trip when I was eighteen years old and continue to this day; my way to keep chaos at bay—binders arranged for each room.*

OENOPHILE'S DELIGHT

Our wine room is much more than just storage for our vintage wines and spirits; it also glows with the warmth of memories of family and friends. The gilt mirror on a formerly empty wall is lined with photos from noteworthy family gatherings, and it is flanked on both sides with framed personal letters from presidents and first ladies (I had the privilege of visiting the White House in both the Clinton and Bush administrations), while antique bar memorabilia from Kevin's father evokes family history. Books on wine and wine regions and my collection of vintage French bistro glasses fill the shelves of an oversized black lacquered cabinet. While this room seamlessly fulfills its mission by storing our chardonnays, Burgundies, and proseccos, it is those personal touches that add character here—even down to the small French cereal bowls, a gift from a friend, personalized with our sons' names, and now the repository of old corks from our favorite wines. For practicality and necessary amenities, we installed an under-the-counter wine cooler, replaced the existing sink with a hand-hammered one, and added a countertop made of a mixture of colorful mosaic tiles that reflects the walls' golden hue. Though originally a rather utilitarian space lacking architectural detail, by mixing keepsakes unique to our family with the essential accessories of any barroom, this space is transformed from the ordinary to the extraordinary and has since become one of our friends' favorite hangouts.

ABOVE: *Family photos are a never-ending and fascinating way to soften the edges of an antique mirror.* **OPPOSITE:** *A corner of our wine room is not only ready for a festive gathering, but it also invites friends to poke around and enjoy our memorabilia. Practical amenities, such as an ice maker and under-the-counter wine cooler, make this room functional as well.*

ABOVE: *A photograph of our slumbering sons when they were younger. Their breakfast cereal bowls from France have a new life as memory-keepers of corks from favorite wine tastings.* **OPPOSITE:** *An open-shelved, painted cabinet makes entertaining easy and elegant with our glasses, pitchers, and carafes nearby.*

ABOVE: *Invitations are arranged chronologically on a wall to keep my family's social commitments organized.* **OPPOSITE, CLOCKWISE FROM UPPER LEFT:** *A cherished gift from my producer at* The Oprah Winfrey Show *contains my many wine stoppers; an oversized Waterford crystal flower vase becomes a gorgeous ice bucket; Kevin's father's leather monogrammed flask holds court above one of his many billiards and sailing awards; I was thrilled when I discovered this vintage champagne-labeled bottle opener, which fits in perfectly with my collection of old and new silver.*

CULINARY ADVENTURES

As a writer of cookbooks and a book on kitchen design, and having had the privilege of interviewing, in the past, many chefs including the late Julia Child, Craig Claiborne, and James Beard—all legendary culinary talents in their own right—I knew immediately what I felt our kitchen needed to make it become the heart of our home—for kitchens, cookbooks (vintage and new), and cooking are three of my many passions. This kitchen had to not only be a place of efficiency and convenience, but it also had to reflect our respect for the history of our home.

With the architectural challenges in its layout as a simple carriage house kitchen, I needed to find just the right backdrop to help unify all of its many angles and corners. Pierre Frey's toile fabric in tangerine and mustard shades seemed a perfect solution. It would coordinate well with the existing golden-toned cabinetry and help to give the room a fanciful French farmhouse feel that I wanted to maintain. I painted practically every other existing surface, including the ceiling, which helped immensely with its harmonious transformation.

To make the small space feel larger, I employed an old design trick of covering the walls with an assortment of picture frames. I knew that my beloved signed menus from favorite restaurants, which have traveled with me over the years, would find the perfect place here—creating almost a mural-like feeling and filling the room with fond memories of special past dining experiences.

An old radiator underneath the window seemed extraneous (and also barely functional), so by removing it, I was able to design and add an L-shaped banquette, reminiscent of one that I had photographed for my book *Kitchens* many years ago.

As I was musing about the banquette's configuration and knowing how little storage and work space I had in this room, I added two lift-up cabinets in the center of the banquette and created two open doggie beds on each end. Their dog-bone cutouts and comfy pillows let our pooches know that this is their space—shared these days with our newest arrival, Dudley, a small but definitely bossy Maltese.

Slipper chairs, another one of my signature design touches, surround our table. The result is that at least six people can easily gather around this table (or around our larger antique pine one) when Kevin or I are inspired to try out a new recipe—helping to make this space truly a room of gustatory delights and simple pleasures.

OPPOSITE: *A reproduction of a train-station clock and extra shelving for glassware separate the pantry area from our kitchen banquette and work area, home to our dogs, guests, and chefs—usually Kevin and me.*

ABOVE: *A late-afternoon still life.* **OPPOSITE:** *When the mood and crowd call for it, I'll change out our small circular table for this farmhouse pine table.*

ABOVE: *Our two Westies immediately fell in love with the L-shaped banquette I designed with cubbies for them at either end.*
OPPOSITE: *Chef-signed menus from great restaurants (and meals) around the world make our walls come alive with fond memories.*

PART II
GATHERINGS

CHARMED LIVING

Walking through our home for the first time, its appeal and bygone-era sensibility totally captivated me, but I wasn't prepared for the evocative feel the living room exuded.

As a fervent devotee of symmetrical spaces, I can honestly say that this room certainly was not, to say the least, symmetrical, nor would decorating it be a simple task. The word "daunting" is more what came to mind, but it was clear to me that the living room both anchored and added a distinct architectural sense to our rambling carriage house.

In my mind's eye that day, as I wandered around the room, I could easily envision how the original tenants, nearly a hundred years ago, gathered here after a day of hard work to perhaps sit down, put their feet up, and maybe even sip a favorite drink or two in front of most likely their only source of heat—a roaring fire.

In much the same way, these days Kevin and I seem to gravitate to this unpretentious room at the end of our occasionally long days, with guests, family, or sometimes just our three dogs as company to re-create—a century later—that sense of contentment, reflection, and relaxation.

I wanted our living room to be functional and aesthetically pleasing, so I divided, or "zoned," the room into four separate seating areas—a difficult challenge since this room is not, by today's standards, overly large, but I felt this configuration

of multiple seating choices would allow for both intimate conversations and for more expansive party gatherings.

Because I'm an admirer of more monochromatic and soothing color schemes—especially in living rooms—I worked out a new color palette that

PREVIOUS SPREAD: *An overview of our living room with its woven wool carpet laid on the pattern's diagonal, which helps to unify the room's unusual shape. The English leather-and-wood sofa table provides needed display space and divides the room into different seating areas, while an unusual desk of unknown origin sits beneath four antique astrological prints from Paris.*
ABOVE: *The original oak doors open into our living room with a view of our ever-changing mantel.* OPPOSITE: *An inviting spot at the end of a winter's day. Accoutrements such as a warm woolen throw, a good book, a plate of clementines, and plenty of firewood in an antique mustard-colored tin container seem to always draw us in here.*

would coordinate with my existing fabrics, incorporating all those hues of stone, pewter, gold, cream, and light brown that permeate this space with an inviting and "come in and sit down" sensibility. A wool diamond-patterned rug—which runs on the diagonal and is bound in a chocolate-brown leather—helps to unify the unusual architectural elements while visually lightening the room.

And with this room's new layout in mind, I decided on a love seat, rather than a larger sofa, which seats two comfortably and faces our room's focal point—the fireplace—which can be either roaring or filled with a lush fern plant or hydrangea, depending on the season. Along with our comfortably laid-back "French '40s" club chairs in a modern version of a Jacobean pattern and a pair of undersized barrel chairs, this grouping forms a central gathering spot surrounding the hearth.

Bookcases at either end of the room—a set of built-ins flanking the fireplace and, at the opposite end, a pair of freestanding bookcases—accommodate my collection of rare, first-edition, and autographed books. Over the years, that seemingly simple act of having an author or friend inscribe a book has added immense and incalculable pleasure to my life.

One of my first antique purchases many years ago was a fruitwood chest, which currently rests against one wall and is filled on top with a large assortment of papier-mâché *objets* I love to collect. It has traveled with me just about everywhere, and I always seem to find the right spot for that piece. A wood and leather-topped English sofa table (circa 1880) helps divide the room and provides us with much-needed space for additional lighting; atop, matching beige gourd-shaped lamps with their drum shades add just the right touch of modernity, which I think the room needed.

A serendipitous find in Vermont, and a fitting one, was a gray velvet pillow, embroidered with a key, the symbol of my life and business philosophy for over three decades. The key represents my belief that the key to successful decorating is turning one's home into a personal haven—certainly true for my family and me—and the pillow's design adds character to this down-filled settee, helping to create a great room for living.

ABOVE: *I glimpsed this barrel-shaped chair in an upholsterer's store window, and covered it in a plush wool mohair with nail-head trim. The fabric of an Aubusson pillow, found in London's Camden Passage many years ago, includes the room's many chocolate and golden hues. The painting is by a nineteenth-century landscape artist.* OPPOSITE: *The settee's design adds character to one side of our living room.*

ABOVE: *One of my favorite writers signed her book,* Paradise.
OPPOSITE: *A timeless and continuously expanding collection of treasured books by cherished writers.*

RIGHT: *Looking from the fireplace toward the front hall and stone dining area. The cream-and-chocolate pillows along with gourd lamps on the table behind add a contemporary touch to the room's ambiance.*

new american living rooms

Bierenberg   **NEW FRENCH COUNTRY**

Jeffrey Bilhuber *defining* LUXURY

RIGHT: *The luminescence of old and new silver pieces dresses up our pair of antique mirrored coffee tables.* **FOLLOWING SPREAD, CLOCKWISE FROM UPPER LEFT:** *Collected over the years—papier-mâché objets in all shapes and sizes; some of my miniature and amusing dogs; a silver tea set; 33⅓ rpm vinyl records are played on a new version of a '50s-era record player.*

One decorating touch that brings color and life to any room is a rich-looking flower arrangement. Whether loosely arranged or tightly packed, blossoms and berries and even weeds and leaves can complement the design aesthetic as well as add visual interest, texture, and aromatic appeal. An added bonus for me, I've discovered that the simple act of cutting flowers from the garden early in the morning or in the evening after sundown is a perfect way to relax and unwind.

The task of creating that pleasing grouping can sometimes be a challenge and require, I've found, a little bit of experimentation and a lot of inspiration! When selecting flowers, I'll visually "check" the space first—thinking about the wall color, window treatments, and furnishings. In a neutrally toned area, as in my own living room, I love all colors and their unexpected punch can change the mood of any space—so I might choose parrot tulips or sunflowers in the kitchen, rust cabbage roses in the living room, but usually a calming neutral bouquet for our bedrooms.

Also remember that proportion is key. I try to select a container based on where it will be placed; I use everything from small jelly jars and vintage milk bottles to antique and unusually shaped holders, such as old French toile lunch boxes. I love some leaves or petals trailing over the

sides. I also like to tear out images of gorgeous flower arrangements from design magazines for inspiration. This practice can be so helpful when faced with a plethora of flowers from my garden.

I'm also fortunate to have a multitude of gardens, and with the help of Mike Murphy and his team, each one serves a distinct purpose—from my kitchen vegetable and herb garden to my early spring garden with snow drops, crocuses, and bleeding hearts pushing up to my beloved rose garden, with all of its varieties to teach me patience, while luring me outside each morning.

ABOVE: *An unexpected pleasure, flowers and cheeses in the same festive hues.* **OPPOSITE, CLOCKWISE FROM UPPER LEFT:** *Garden peonies and roses in a favorite export-ware pitcher; simple garden rhododendrons make a great impact when placed in a toile container; a party setup is enhanced by an understated floral arrangement; a mix of early spring gatherings from my garden sit atop an old but treasured papier-mâché table inlaid with mother-of-pearl (with our dog Winnie underneath).*

Past and Present Pleasures

When we moved into our home, I was presented with a difficult design dilemma—namely, how to deal with what was essentially a nondescript, narrow walk-through that linked our garage entryway to the kitchen. It was an awkward space, to say the least, but one that I suspected, if reconfigured, could become both functional and inviting for our family, friends, and, of course, pets.

While I was deciding what to make of this space, I thought, "Where do most families gather these days?" So thinking about my immediate and extended family of nieces, nephews, and close friends, I realized that they—like many others—seem to gravitate to an area that combines all those activities that bring us together for leisurely pursuits in our sometimes frantic and fast-paced lives.

I began to envision this as an informal family room with game boards, music, books, and television—in other words, a room for casual relaxing and

watching movies, where our three dogs would also be welcome with us on a sofa. As luck would have it, a sectional I designed over a decade ago fit seamlessly against two exterior walls, thus allowing me to slide our oversized television into a niche that was created on the opposite wall—an attraction for my sons and their friends during football, basketball, and baseball seasons (are there any others?)

ABOVE: *In a small closet I was able to create an organized spot for one of my passions—music. The CDs are arranged and labeled according to their genre.* OPPOSITE: *The hand-rubbed beige walls, rug, and upholstered furniture ground the room's wood furniture, allowing displays of framed family photographs, books, and other decorative pieces to stand out.*

and for Kevin and me to DVR our favorite shows and news programs and to unwind with those old black-and-white movies that we love.

We reupholstered our old sectional with a sturdy but elegant-looking, diamond-patterned beige chenille fabric, and added the punch of azure blue and dark coffee-colored pillows in a modern geometric pattern. Inserting a double-tiered coffee table with two matching side pieces helped to organize all those piles of books, magazines, and scrapbooks while giving me tabletops to display family photographs.

And because I'm an inveterate collector of found objects and artifacts, vintage horticulture books, and an assemblage of other natural treasures, an oversized cabinet with antiqued chicken wire that I designed many years ago turned out to be just the right scale and color to house my *objets* in a corner of our now "newly created" family room. Besides forming a rich backdrop to an empty wall and giving the narrow room a greater feeling of depth, these personal touches lend the space a sense of our family's history.

PREVIOUS SPREAD: *A family room—often used— that reflects a full life of family trips, gatherings of friends, and hotly contested board games, and that houses a well-disguised large-screen television.* RIGHT: *At the end of this room and up a few steps is our family's informal entryway. Original and early Alfred Birdsey paintings, serendipitously discovered and bought while on a morning jog during a hotel's demolition, hang on the right wall.*

ABOVE: *Another early design of mine, a bibliothèque, or bookcase, holds several collections—each with a unifying color scheme, including a collection found at our local library's book sale of the* Library of Universal History, *original glass specimen jars, and shells of varying shapes and sizes.* **OPPOSITE:** *A detail of one of the shelves. I love how all the elements naturally work together.*

ERS of
...uitoc, DC.
...ZIL.
...RY Esq. F.R.S

...NAGA, Linn.
...tuills from Africa
...making root plates of the
...Bromfield

Impa...
and the...

MISCELLANIES

LIBRA
OF
UNIVER
HIST

Fragrant flowers of Mesua
BOMBAY.
1877.   C. CHANTRE E...

"BIYAKUSHI."
Angelica sylvestris, L.
Used in medicine in Japan.
HIOGO.

W. A. WOOLLEY, Esq.

ABOVE: *An oversized and sturdy basket holds some of my overflow of books.*
OPPOSITE, CLOCKWISE FROM UPPER LEFT: *Details make a home into a haven: binoculars alongside a nautilus shell and a 1905 signed photograph of Kevin's grandfather's first sailboat; vintage and colorful Chinese checkers and board; a wooden Buddha holds coins from a previous trip to Hong Kong, along with a good-luck key and tassel from my first furniture collection; a decoupaged tray on our entry-hall table holds recent mail.*

PART III

REPOSE AND REJUVENATION

AFTERNOON LIGHT

One of the pleasures of our home is that—although not large in terms of square footage—it is blessed with a plethora of smaller, interesting spaces, each with its own character and, I think, panache.

By adding a wall and door to separate a narrow, long anteroom from our bedroom, I was able to create a sitting room. Filled with sunlight from the oversized windows, the room is a quiet setting for our morning coffee and newspaper reading, before we head downstairs to greet the vagaries of the day, review our e-mails, and walk our three dogs. The space's subdued color palette and needlepoint leopard pillows make it a favorite morning spot of mine after I finish my yoga practice.

I try not to do any business "work" in this sitting area, so my chinoiserie armoire-cum-desk, which I designed years ago in the Philippines, houses my large array of stationery and my assortment of calligraphy pens—necessary tools for my never-ending goal to stay abreast of my personal correspondence. Like the rest of the world, I'm an avid e-mailer, but I constantly strive to handwrite as many notes as possible. I love receiving personal letters—I think we all do.

A particularly distinctive piece—a seventeenth-century Venetian chest that I discovered on one of my antiquing "hunts"—is placed against one wall, and its narrow top (I added a cream marble slab to make it a bit sturdier and to soften its darker wood

tones) holds some of the many pieces of silver I've collected over the years, as well as photographs of family and close friends. Incorporating these personal touches in a formerly walk-through area helped to set the stage for our bedroom—creating a relaxing ambiance that I know we all strive for these days.

PREVIOUS SPREAD: *Silk buffalo-check balloon shades frame the bay window in our sitting room overlooking the garden.* ABOVE: *A favorite afternoon napping and sitting area with a view of the attached and original stone carriage house.* OPPOSITE: *A quiet moment for me.* FOLLOWING SPREAD: *Underneath the strong foundation of an oversized mirror is a small but comfortable Napoleon III settee covered in a relaxed beige linen. Animal prints, especially leopard, abound throughout my life—here in pillows from a late friend, Lyn Hoyt.*

ABOVE: *A detail of one of the pieces from my accessories collection—an elephant created entirely of resin.* **OPPOSITE:** *Landings, if large enough, allow for decorating creatively; a small settee complete with faux-zebra-skin pillows and a deliberately undressed window brighten the space.*

ABOVE: *One of my first furniture designs created with Matt Johnson—a chinoiserie secretary.* **OPPOSITE:** *From the Tang Museum's modern silver "bird's nest" to antique Tiffany trays, baby rattles, picture frames, and table accoutrements, all are balanced by the teapot and server, while the glass tray behind reflects their luminescent patinas.*

SWEET DREAMS

What is it about bedrooms that makes so many of us want to create soft, intimate, and soothing settings, whether contemporary, country, traditional, or, sometimes, even thematic?

Is it because we spend countless hours here—some say a third of our lives for those lucky ones—or perhaps because it is the last visual image we see in the evening and the first in the morning? Or is it because we need to refresh our bodies and soothe our souls, and this setting is often the perfect milieu to do so? I think it may also be because bedrooms evoke memories from our youth.

Our bedroom addressed all of these needs and went a bit further. Fortunately, the previous owners seamlessly added a two-story addition to our original carriage house: upstairs, a spacious double-height master-bedroom suite with a large anteroom, which we later converted to two rooms—a sitting room, and my meditation and yoga space—while below on the first level is the garage.

This generously proportioned bedroom, with its soaring ceiling and large windows on two sides, has a distinctly different atmosphere than the charming yet small "English cottage with a bit of French farmhouse" ambiance of the rest of the house. Sometimes, when I wake up in the morning in this sun-filled room with vistas of our rose gardens (or snow mounds) outside the windows, I feel like a very lucky princess without the pea—content in the ethereal surroundings that envelop me.

I grew up on Long Island in a large family of eleven and often shared a room with my younger and very artistic sister Mary Beth. My parents—in retrospect—were very indulgent of my plans to decorate and redecorate our bedroom with various color schemes and patterns over the years, and my sister was also quite forgiving of my need to imagine our beds as boats, rafts, or even spaceships, as the princess (guess who?) escaped from imaginary pirates and monsters.

And so in designing my sons' bedrooms as they were growing up—and in the various evolutions of my husband, Kevin's, and my bedrooms—comfort, convenience, and style (plus a plethora of pillows in all shapes and sizes) were key.

The color palette of the fabric that I chose

OPPOSITE: *Matelassé area rugs underfoot unify our aerie-inspired upstairs—the bedroom and sitting rooms—while creating a strong juxtaposition to the darker furniture pieces that we've collected over the years.*

with Toni Gallagher is a calming cream and robin's-egg blue, and although I wanted this luxe fabric everywhere, reality and budget wisely intruded. I kept the cream silk curtains that came with the house, adding a glass button trim, and upholstered my curbside treasures of a dressing table and banquette, which fit nicely at the far end of the room.

An antique Chinese cupboard, formerly in our office, tucked into the niche opposite our bed, holds our CDs and tapes, television, and DVDs of old movies.

Since I enjoy being surrounded by books, they are absolutely everywhere—in our built-in bookcases, as well as piled high on and slipped under benches and small side tables I've collected just for this purpose. They are, quite literally, spilling out, it seems some days, from everywhere.

And, finally, for me, a wish from my childhood was fulfilled with a wall-attached canopy covered with that same robin's-egg-blue–patterned fabric, which helps to ensure sweet dreams.

RIGHT: *A glass chandelier, hung slightly lower than usual in our oversized bedroom area, continues the light and harmonious sensibility, while the patterned linens from Carlton V unify the room's different shades of cream, taupe, and beige.*

ABOVE: *The Jansen mirrored night table with a mixture of frames—all in silver—evokes family memories. The bed linens from my bedding collection at JCPenney are monogrammed and add some personalized embellishment and contrast to the nail-head and softly woven headboard.*
OPPOSITE: *A trip to New Orleans and its historic city museum many years ago is where I discovered this oval, beribboned gilt-wood mirror, and it complements my antique metal picture frames perfectly. The soft drape of the original silk-taffeta curtains are reflected in the mirrored top of my dressing table—found, by me, in the trash on the streets of New York City.*

ABOVE: *Another curbside discovery—a French settee reupholstered and button-tufted—fits in the far end of our bedroom, creating a cozy yet understated corner.* **OPPOSITE:** *A duchesse brisée, a two-piece French chair, is an ideal reading (or napping) spot surrounded by a background of memories.*

and microwave are all easily accessible and provide us with a small but much appreciated luxury on those days when time is of the essence.

This practical touch to the otherwise sublime atmosphere of our bedroom allows us the convenience of grabbing an occasional midnight snack without having to leave the comfort of our bedroom (or wake up the doggies!). It is an easily duplicated design trick for any bedroom. How easy was that!

One of my favorite features in our master bedroom is a customized breakfast bar, cleverly hidden in one of our armoires, which I had designed several years ago. With the spatial and structural limitations of the piece in mind, I strategically outfitted it with all the necessities for morning coffee or tea, fruit, and a croissant plus a ready supply of napkins, flatware, an antique breakfast set, and some extra coffee and tea cups nearby. A coffeemaker, refrigerator,

PREVIOUS SPREAD: *A pair of Gothic-inspired armoires are practical, yet in keeping with the ambiance of our private quarters. The interior of our armoire on the right serves as our quick-and-easy breakfast nook, while the piece on the left is for storing travel items and other paraphernalia.* **ABOVE:** *The inner workings of our armoire.* **OPPOSITE:** *The creamware set ready for morning tea.*

ABOVE: *A detail of happy memories and sports photography.* **RIGHT:** *The bedroom of our youngest son, Nick, is relatively intact for his occasional visits home. Although darker, with more masculine tones, it is in keeping with the rest of our house, with animal prints, plaids, multiple pillows, and, of course, his favorite memorabilia.*

RIGHT: *A touch of Monet's Giverny garden—one of my favorite places on the outskirts of Paris to visit with my sister—inspired the blue-and-white-with-a-pop-of-yellow color scheme in our guest bedroom. The flowered wall covering is simply curtains that have been cut and stapled to the wall, with white roping glued around the edges. Night tables, lamps, bedding, and some floral-patterned blue plates—created by me—work seamlessly with our twin antique four-poster beds.*

PAMPERING ESSENTIALS

How can a bathroom make one fall in love with a house?

For me, after a childhood of sharing two family baths with eight siblings (as much fun as it was), I have always longed for a room with a view for my daily ablutions. When I first walked into this space, I knew it was, for me, "bathroom nirvana," since the tub rests beneath a huge window (seven-by-six feet) and the bathroom was complete with an antique chandelier and a very modern shower with steam and sauna.

In my research for one of my earlier books, I learned that the Romans had painted the walls of their "latrines" with deities and other hallowed emblems for protection, so I decided to cover my tall walls over the tub with some of my favorite prints, taken by admired photographers, such as Penn, Avedon, Arbus, and Greene. The black-and-white photographs—each of the female

form in various guises—are all inspirational to me in the midst of a long bubble bath at the end of an equally long day!

I decided to add color with a rainbow of Porthault towels, which complement the pale-yellow Jerusalem limestone that covers so much of our bathroom floor and walls.

I was also able to create a small breakfast nook and vanity area with a beautiful antiqued, japanned, and mirrored trifold cabinet with drawers beneath for makeup paraphernalia.

On the other hand, our two powder rooms downstairs follow my design dictum of making little water closets into small gems with unexpected objects of interest—besides their functional use and necessities for guests.

Their assemblages are remembrances of places and friends—guaranteed to add panache and style to any environment, but especially the powder room.

ABOVE: *Flowers can add a sense of well-being to any space but especially to my bathroom.* **OPPOSITE:** *The house's previous owners graciously left behind our bathroom's overhead chandelier, which makes this room glow at night—full moon or not—and the oversized, strategically placed windows allow me the luxury of privacy while gazing at the stars above during a long soak. Fabric-covered hat boxes hold all sorts of bath accoutrements. Black-and-white prints of iconic women, taken by equally iconic photographers, gracefully cover the walls.*

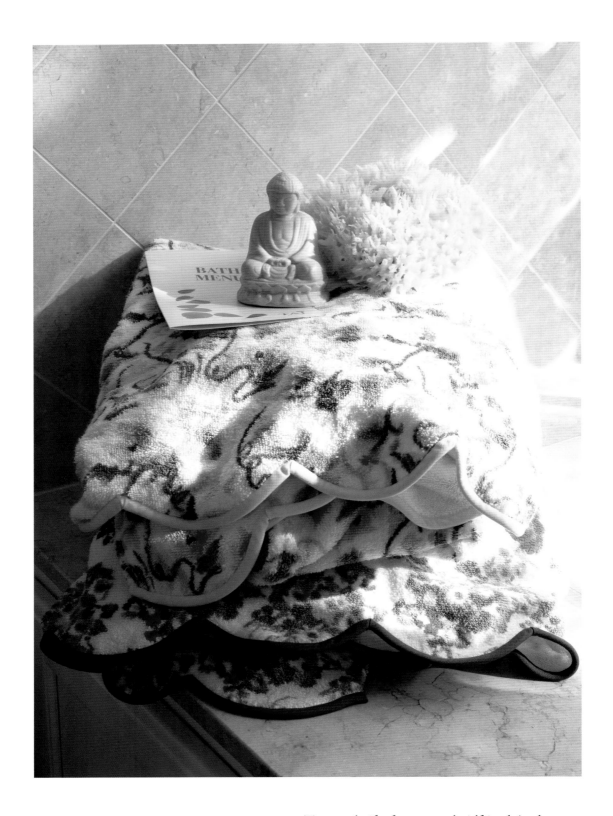

ABOVE: *Treasured gifts from a good girlfriend (and a great designer and shopkeeper), Lynn von Kersting, Porthault towels and a Buddha soap rest in a corner of my tub's surround.*
OPPOSITE: *The yellow undertones of the Jerusalem limestone are a soothing counterpoint to the ebony black of my antique dressing table, diminutive lamp shades, and Wedgwood breakfast set.*

Be yourself.
There is something
that you can do
better than any other.
Listen to the inward voice
and bravely...

ABOVE: *A ruby-red powder room was inspired by the color of a simple red hand towel.* OPPOSITE: *The sink skirt of red-and-gold baroque fabric adds instant age to this small space.*

ABOVE: *Another find—Ginny Bauer created these paper hand towels using the wallpaper's circular motif.* **OPPOSITE:** *A favorite pattern of mine—treillage and teahouses—adds a bit of whimsy to a previously dark powder room with black appointments.*

PART IV

PRIVATE SANCTUARIES

MY RENAISSANCE ROOM

Ever since I embarked on my journey for my book (which then turned into a television special) entitled *A Room of Her Own: Women's Personal Spaces*—almost fifteen years ago—scores of women have asked me about the origin of this little room created for me and by me.

Almost two decades ago, in our previous house, I designed a small space to meditate in and do my morning yoga practice and to prepare myself for the day's demands, and I dedicated it to the memory of my younger sister Patty. I found it to be a true place of comfort and solace, and created a similar space in our carriage house. Here I began to add places for more of my passions—painting, music, and photography—making it a room, a sanctuary, where I could, as Katherine Hepburn once said, "refill the reservoir."

The two cabinets I designed for my first furniture collection became repositories for my collection of old tapes from yoga teachers throughout the world, and my containers of incense, candles, and oils truly help me gravitate to this little corner of my life each morning. Of course, my "do not disturb" sign keeps the outside world at bay till I've completed my morning rituals—difficult to attain in our time-sensitive world, but a concept that I have tried to practice daily, no matter where I am, for over three decades.

And the view of my rose gardens outside my windows, beyond the desk of my design and named "Colette" (after one of my favorite writers), certainly brings me a sense of rejuvenation as I prepare for my day to unfold in so many different and often unexpected ways.

PREVIOUS SPREAD: *Some of my most cherished objects surround my first typewriter.* **RIGHT:** *Previously a deep green tone, these two cabinets were lightened up with a fresh coat of cream paint, which made them fit in rather than stand out in my morning centering space. Wheatgrass, a portable easel, and a yoga mat, along with a leopard-pattern bench, give the room all the color it needs.*

ABOVE: *A glimpse into a private corner of my personal space. As I encourage all women during my seminars—these mementos need only be special to you.* **OPPOSITE:** *A detail of my "Colette" desk with glass globes, wheatgrass, and an inspirational painting by a Caribbean artist.*

KEVIN'S PERSONAL RETREAT

lthough I have often written and lectured on the subject of "personal spaces" and how I feel strongly that each of us in this fast-paced and oftentimes stressful world should have a sanctuary or retreat, or even a corner of his or her own, I confess that my original concept of "personal space" was directed primarily to women, so I was surprised (although, in retrospect, I probably shouldn't have been) at the number of men who shared with me their need to have their own place, too—away from the demands of the day.

So, I was excited about creating one solely for Kevin in what was originally a walk-through space with enormous closets. I decided to remove them and add a wall of bookcases around the doorway and high hats, along with some standing lamps for ambiance and reading.

Anchored by a dramatic leopard-skin carpet that runs throughout these upper rooms and staircases, his room is filled with books (many of them paperbacks since he loves keeping his favorites nearby), family photographs, his sports team photos from prep school and college, a marvelous

antique bar (disguised as an enormous globe of the world), and, of course, a flat-screen television for those NFL Sundays . . . and Mondays.

A small love seat against one wall (the space formerly occupied by the closets) is perfect for reading and recharging. In front of it is an old and distressed butler's tray table, which I found and lowered by sawing off its legs to make it coffee-

table height, piled with more books and our collection of vintage political buttons.

For me, it's always amusing to see how many of our male friends gravitate upstairs to this room (referred to by some as a "man cave") for a modern-day take on brandy and cigars, after dinner in our dining room these many enlightened years later!

ABOVE: *A reconfigured butler's tray table is a fanciful place to display some of our button collection.* **OPPOSITE:** *To each his own—Kevin's study is filled with many of his mementos, from cigars and sports paraphernalia to family photographs and books.*

ABOVE: *Unusually designed but very practical bookshelves were built floor to ceiling around the perimeter of the doorway leading to my office; they follow the idiosyncratic footprint and sloping ceilings of our carriage house.*
OPPOSITE: *A timeless pattern, leopard works well in so many guises. Here, it unites and updates our almost hundred-year-old staircase and adjoining rooms.*

I began my company in a small home office, and now—thirty-plus years later—even though I have a staff and an outside office, I still find I need a space where I have the luxury of working, sewing, scanning and printing my photographs, and writing when the spirit moves me; I like to call it my "creative refuge."

An inveterate sewer since childhood, I carved out a small nook in this room where I can while away hours designing and sewing. This modest yet well-proportioned space gives me that freedom—and certainly comes in handy when under deadlines! My oversized file drawers hold my netbook on one side with plenty of storage

in the open cabinets overhead.

Today's technology oftentimes requires that we are reachable 24/7, but by having this functional space far from my more personal and family-oriented rooms, I have found that I can lose myself in here—creating to my heart's content.

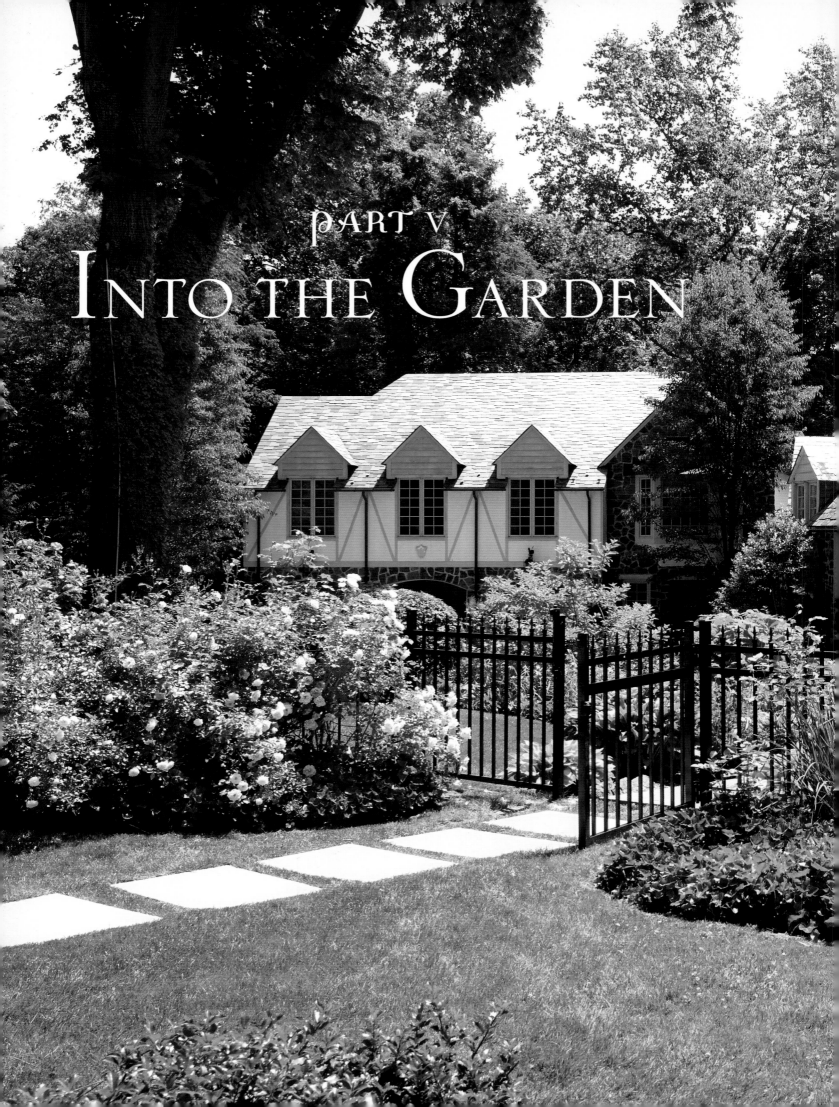

PART V
INTO THE GARDEN

AL FRESCO ENTICEMENTS

Summertime—and the living is easy, but as we all know, a well-tended garden doesn't come naturally. And as our Northeastern winter days become longer and suggestions of spring permeate the air, I find myself outside seeing what survived our winter and making a mental list of what I might be looking for on my next visit to my local nursery. I'm a lover of perennials since they never fail my gardens or me, but I always seem to find some new annual that will give these areas just the punch of color or scent that they need—Moroccan lavender, lilies, butterfly bushes, cabbage and climbing roses continue to delight, while the latest colors in impatiens for my shady walkways and petunias and pansies are instant pick-me-ups for those spots that are always a gardener's challenge come spring. My greenhouse helps immensely and has become a destination for me even in the midst of winter, but it's when I'm out in the gardens, pruning, photographing, or simply coaxing along a neglected corner of the outdoor landscape that I find true contentment.

One of my favorite activities in those warm spring and summer months in our neck of the woods is to entertain friends and family by our pool, which is surrounded by these gardens. The pool itself is of an old-fashioned rectangular shape—built in the late '60s—recalling the old-style pools of Hollywood, with its clean lines and lack of ornamentation. To make it even more inviting, I designed a cabana with waterproof striped fabric and an inexpensive metal structure found at our local home and garden supply store. It's become one of our favorite outdoor gathering spots—whether for post-pool races or early evening cocktails. Glass containers of candles abound in the evening hours, always an invitation—as when we were children—to stay up "just a little past our bedtime!"

PREVIOUS SPREAD: *Blessed to inherit a vibrant rose garden from the previous owner, I was able to enhance this ethereal setting by adding more sturdy rose bushes that all blossom into full splendor—almost like clockwork—albeit with a bit of work every June and late August.* ABOVE: *A butterfly on a butterfly bush on a hot July afternoon.* OPPOSITE: *A French galvanized container holds some of my favorite lavender blooms.*

ABOVE: *A view of our back terrace and gardens through our dining room's French doors.* **OPPOSITE:** *A simple black metal arched "moon gate" with an attached low fence for our dogs. The back field is deliberately left to grow freely—a deeply pastoral contrast to our many flower gardens.*

RASPBERRY CRÊPES

A perfect summer treat for family and friends, particularly when we would contribute our own fresh raspberries. These light and luscious dessert crêpes can be made in advance and frozen until ready to fill. If you aren't making them ahead of time, prepare the batter the evening before so that it has a chance to settle.

1	cup flour
3	eggs
1¾	cups milk
	Dash of salt
3	tablespoons vegetable oil
1	tablespoon butter, melted
1	tablespoon Curacao rum
1	cup heavy cream
½	teaspoon sugar
1	pint raspberries
	Confectioners' sugar

Mix the flour, eggs, milk, salt, oil, and rum in a large bowl and whisk until smoothly blended. Brush a skillet or crêpe pan with oil and heat over a medium flame. Pour in enough batter to coat the bottom, tilting the pan to help it spread. When the crêpe is lightly browned on the bottom and begins to form tiny bubbles, turn it quickly and brown the other side. Remove to a warm plate. Repeat the process, adding more butter as needed. This makes about 18 crêpes. (Now is the time to freeze them.)

Whip the cream with the sugar until stiff peaks form, and gently fold in the raspberries. Spread the crêpes with the

The SUMMER HOUSE COOKBOOK

Chris Casson Madden

— $5.95 An Original Harvest/HBJ Book —

raspberry and cream mixture and roll up. Dust with confectioners' sugar. Chill before serving.

GARDEN PARTY TEA

C. Z. Guest taught me this recipe many years ago when I visited her world-renowned gardens. It has become a summer entertaining favorite of mine ever since.

6	tea bags
2	quarts water
¼	cup superfine sugar (or more to taste)
1	cup orange juice
6	mint sprigs
½	lemon
1	orange
	Cloves

Make the tea: Either steep the tea bags in boiling water for 3 minutes or set them in jars in the sun or in the refrigerator for several hours. Chill. Before serving, add the sugar, orange juice, and mint sprigs. Slice the lemon and

orange and stick each slice with 3–4 cloves. Put the tea in a punch bowl and float the fruit slices on top. Makes about 10 cups.

MARY MADDEN'S CHEESE BALL

Nana Mare's annual contribution.

2	8-ounce packages cream cheese, at room temperature
1	cup grated Cheddar cheese
½	cup blue or Roquefort cheese
	Dash of Worcestershire sauce
1	tablespoon minced onions
½	teaspoon paprika
1	tablespoon chopped parsley
1	cup chopped pecans
¼	cup chopped parsley

In a food processor or a large bowl, blend together the cream cheese, Cheddar cheese, and blue cheese. Add the Worcestershire, onion, paprika, one tablespoon parsley, and a half cup of the pecans. Place in the refrigerator to harden, then remove and shape into a ball.

Mix together the ¼ cup parsley and the remaining pecans and sprinkle them on a sheet of waxed paper. Roll the cheese ball in this mixture until well covered. Keep wrapped until ready to serve. This recipe will make a very sizable cheese ball. For smaller groups, cut the recipe in half.

*ABOVE: My first book on the pleasures of summertime cooking. **OPPOSITE, CLOCKWISE FROM UPPER LEFT:** Pink-patterned napkins and fresh fruits give my white tableware all the bright color needed; a new addition and one that makes perfect sense in our sunny back terrace is a retractable awning above where we gather for early morning coffee in the warmer months with the newspaper and our dogs as company; pink lemonade with some sprigs of our vigorous and indomitable mint tossed in for added flavor; practical aluminum outdoor furniture is not only comfortable but Ashley Rummel's artistry also helps bring ordinary Sunbrella pillows to life.*

PREVIOUS SPREAD: *My antique wrought-iron furniture just fits under the climbing rose–and– clematis-covered arbor— a perfect spot for afternoon refreshments.*
LEFT: *Dudley, our Maltese, enjoys the late-afternoon sun by the pool.*

ABOVE: *Two chaises are protected from the noonday sun by plenty of greenery overhead in this corner by our old-fashioned pool.* **OPPOSITE, CLOCKWISE FROM UPPER LEFT:** *A vintage pitcher and goblet in milky glass—perfect for iced tea; pink lemonade, on a quilted Indian blanket; fresh peaches—almost a still-life painting themselves—with our summer shell centerpiece; a tray of martini glasses works perfectly for festive summer drinks.* **FOLLOWING SPREAD:** *With shades of blue and taupe as the primary colors, I was able to create an outdoor living room beneath our cabana by the pool.*

OUTDOOR SERENITY

I 've always sought out natural outdoor settings from which to carve out quiet spaces for moments of reflection and rejuvenation. One of my favorite places is an old and heavy stone garden bench tucked away in a corner of our backyard.

In the warmer months, this bucolic niche gives me a place to clear my head, perhaps meditate, breathe in the fresh air, and simply enjoy the natural beauty that surrounds me. Removed from the reminders of my daily commitments and obligations, I find it an easy place in which to immerse myself in this spirit of contemplation. For me, it's like stepping into a painting, complete with its own color and music, giving me license to indulge in so many of my favorite sensory delights—music being one—and my outdoor speakers, disguised as rocks (what a brilliant invention) in the bushes and plantings around our gardens, are able to fill the air with sound depending on my whim that day—from Puccini and Steve Tyrell to Michael Bublé and Norah Jones.

A secluded place for meditation and quiet in the garden, whether at the beginning or end of one's day, is, I've discovered, a superb antidote to today's all-encompassing technological and time-sensitive demands.

ABOVE: *An antique garden chair under a shady evergreen.* **OPPOSITE:** *Whether for reading or capturing a quiet moment, the stone bench is in perfect harmony with its surroundings.*

RIGHT: *My garden of perennials—ferns, hostas, astilbes, and PeeGee hydrangeas—is easy to care for and easy on the eyes.*

ABOVE AND OPPOSITE: *Our sturdy little greenhouse is the perfect spot for planting and growing seedlings, and for tending potted herbs and turning clutches of garden flowers into arrangements. A vintage rattan cart does double duty as an extra workstation and is, to my eye, as visually stunning as my pile of terra-cotta pots and collections of antique watering cans and English garden stools— all adding pleasure to this garden's "inner sanctum," as music wafts through our outdoor speakers; the proximity of the greenhouse to our gardens and back kitchen door makes gathering our herbs and vegetables a true delight for me.* **FOLLOWING SPREAD:** *Our fire pit, assembled by our sons, with its rockers, chairs, and benches, is a great place for larger gatherings in the early, cooler evenings.*

OUR GETAWAY

When my husband, Kevin, and I climbed over four-foot snowbanks to take a peek through the windows of the Vermont home (built circa 1970) that would eventually become our family's getaway, I had, as I recall, an instantaneous vision of a dramatically different decorating aesthetic. The house's bones were definitely mired in mid-century-modern architecture, and even its remaining furnishings echoed that sensibility. It was love at first sight, but it quickly became obvious to us that the house needed a much more twenty-first-century approach to comfort and warmth—rather than the coolness of the '50s "hip look."

Having been aficionados of Vermont since the early 1970s, Kevin and I were very well-versed in Vermont culture (and real estate) and immediately knew that this wonderful setting was where we wanted to put down roots for our family's getaway—and so we did—in this former apple orchard overlooking the villages of Manchester and Dorset in southern Vermont.

I had a very definite and passionate knowledge about and fondness for this part of Vermont, having also been a consultant, writing promotional copy and radio commercials for *Blair & Country Journal*, which

PREVIOUS SPREAD: *Spending time with our two West Highland Terrier dogs, Winnie and Lola, on the hillside of our Vermont getaway.*
ABOVE: *Early springtime in Vermont.* OPPOSITE: *Late wintertime in Vermont.*

immersed me in the unique lifestyle of this region—a lively four-season community with outdoor sports, great summer stock theater, fly-fishing, and a sophisticated array of restaurants with world-class chefs.

Our house is one level, and it is perfectly sited on one of the highest points in the village to ably weather those four-foot-plus blizzards in winter and to bask in the cooling mountain breezes of late spring and summer.

And, as with our primary house, I knew that to create a dwelling of warmth and comfort, without sacrificing its architectural integrity, I had to take a step back to analyze our home's layout—an intriguing and, to say the least, challenging project.

I knew that the pink and green metallic wallpaper (among other '70s remnants) and the bright pink living room carpeting would have to go. So once the room was down to its bare bones, I looked at it with a fresh eye, and realized that the brick fireplace and the rustic wooden mantel, along with the room's structural beams and its painted barn siding, gave me a great canvas to build upon. I will always be grateful to the architect, the late Bud Lench, for his timeless sensibility, which allowed us to create our perfect country escape.

ABOVE: *A handcrafted stone wall by a talented landscape architect, Liz Miller, surrounds our home's western exposure and works well as a natural divide between the apple orchards, meadows, and mountains beyond.*

ABOVE: *A view from the moss-covered crab apple trees toward our front door.* **OPPOSITE:** *Vintage milk jugs echo the green of our screen door and frame our winter supply of aged firewood.*

PART I

WEEKEND RETREAT

WALKING STICKS AND COUNTRY HATS

Our Vermont entryway is classically utilitarian and functional—its architect, Bud Lench, was influenced by much of Frank Lloyd Wright's early work—so the house has strong lines and deep overhangs that protect it from the often unpredictable Vermont elements. We not only added durable slate flooring but also a bit of romance with an antique faux-Regency bamboo hat rack and chests (for keeping flashlights, gloves, keys, and dog whistles always accessible), which help set the tone and character for the rest of the house—a more cozy sensibility than most austere mid-century-modern dwellings—as it opens onto our great room, the center and gathering place of our mountain getaway for family and friends.

As one approaches the exterior, the walkway's irregular slate steps soften the linear architecture while creating a rustically charming ambiance. Its sturdy plantings of old crab apple trees and a herbaceous border surrounding the stone walkway and meadows lead up to the front door and an ingenious firewood stacking storage shed (with an interior door for easy reach from inside on snowy days). Resting in front of the wood shed are a pair of vintage metal milk containers—found by me on the side of a road during one of my country drives, with a note that said, in true Vermont fashion, "free—take me home," which I promptly did.

The original and gently faded two-tone green paint of those oversized jugs was the inspiration for the shade of deep green that I painted our front door. Holiday bells on an old leather harness strap hang year-round on that same door, alerting us—and our dogs—to guests' arrivals.

Since the house was built in the early '70s, it has sliding glass doors—a popular design detail during that period—that lead out from the wall opposite the front entry to the decks that surround much of the home. It is, we realized, ironically, quite similar to our main residence's carriage house architecture, both of which allow one to view, through their glass windows and doors, back and front lawns and gardens and fields simultaneously. The glass doors provide a constantly changing canvas of the verdant Vermont countryside, with its magical mountains and valleys.

PREVIOUS SPREAD: *Guests arrive through our screen-door front entry, getting a glimpse of our disparate collections—from the practical to the exotic.* **OPPOSITE:** *Summer straw hats—discovered on trips from Venice to our local garden shop—along with flower-gathering baskets and walking sticks, are a practical welcome for both guests and family.*

A ROOM FOR ALL SEASONS

In some ways our Vermont house, with its "great room"—an oversized, modern space encompassing living, dining, entertaining, and cooking—is the antithesis of our carriage house, with its intimate rooms and nooks and crannies.

This gathering spot in our home in Vermont, which measures thirty feet by twenty-two feet, with its floor-to-ceiling windows and a rustic brick fireplace, makes it truly the place our family loves to congregate. Anchored at one end by bookshelves and a game table and at the other end by a pair of open shelves, which are filled with some of my favorite collections of blue-and-white exportware, this large space is zoned for dining, playing board games, gazing at a roaring fire, or simply hanging out, as well as for celebrating with family and friends.

Our eight-foot-long dining table, with an antique tavern bench and a high-backed settee, is illuminated by a faux-antler chandelier of resin. Center stage in this room is an overstuffed sofa juxtaposed with two club chairs that have served us well since our first apartment. In the winter, the chairs are covered in a cozy wool plaid of blue, tan, and rust shades, which pick up the myriad colors of the brick fireplace. The clover leaf–shaped ottoman is the ideal après-ski spot for curling up in front of the burning hearth—a constant during the winter months. Yet in the warm summer months, I cover all the upholstery in white cotton-denim slipcovers—a trick I learned from the talented, late designer James Amster during my scholarship days at the Fashion Institute of Technology.

The correct lighting in any space is key, but especially in a larger room, so, in addi-

ABOVE: Kevin's favorite chair is situated to catch the early morning sunlight as it rises over the mountains. OPPOSITE: With a view from our fireplace to our front-door entryway, one feels immediately at home with my washable and dog-proof white-denim summer slipcovers and a plethora of pillows in all manner of patterns—part of our great room's informal and relaxed charm.

tion to the oversized chandelier, the structural beams overhead contain modern track-lighting fixtures, while the sofa table holds a pair of armillary-sphere brass lamps that I designed years ago.

I anchored the ends of the refectory table with two woven Chinese wedding baskets (I love their design and history), and an armoire on the opposite wall has been refitted as a modern-day bar for large crowds and our occasional potluck suppers.

Since we are a family of passionate art and photography collectors, the room's high walls allow us to display some of our favorites, including an early Alfred Birdsey painting, a Michael Graves lithograph, a pastel of one of my favorite gardens in Vermont—the Hoyt gardens at the nearby historic Hildene house—and an early-1970s painting by my sister Mary Beth of my husband, Kevin, and me at our first "real" getaway on Long Island, New York—a nod to our present getaway's mid-century roots.

PREVIOUS SPREAD: *Our dogs' wicker bed fits perfectly underneath our antique walnut table.* RIGHT: *Blue and white create a light atmosphere in the great room for the summer months.*

RIGHT: *Even our formal Sheraton sofa gets its own summer slipcover—a scalloped-edged paisley cotton. The binoculars and telescope never seem to stay in one place.*

EPICUREAN ESSENTIALS

There's something very liberating about cooking in a kitchen that opens directly into a larger space, as our Vermont kitchen does, located in the middle of all the action at one end of our great room.

Whether alone or enjoying an evening with family and friends, I'm passionate about cooking and devising recipes in this well-positioned corner, where I am fortunate enough to be able to simultaneously see our fireplace, listen to music, and gaze out at the Green Mountains beyond.

Our Vermont slate countertop, with its U-shaped design, and rattan chairs allow our guests to pull up to the counter and get into the spirit of the kitchen area—and sometimes even to assist as sous chefs, as we boil up lobsters in the summer or indulge in exotically creative fondues in the winter! It's also a perfect setting for packing a picnic basket for a morning hike, serving a hearty pre-ski breakfast, or preparing goodies for a jaunt to our favorite swimming hole—the local quarry.

One wall is outfitted with simple, clean-lined stainless-steel appliances and a smooth glass

cooktop, and what is especially pleasing to me in this open kitchen is that we were able to keep—that is, to recycle—the original fruitwood cabinets, which we then updated with some handsome nickel pulls and a fresh coat of paint swiped with furniture oil. My braided ropes of garlic and vintage copper pots hang over the cooktop—located under the custom hood with its hidden lighting and exhaust (vital in an open kitchen)—lending a sense of ease and personality to this favorite gathering space. Or, to quote from a page in the life of the late Pearl Bailey: "My kitchen is a mystical place, a kind of temple for me. It is a place where the surfaces seem to have significance, where the sounds and odors carry meaning that transfers from the past and bridges to the future."

ABOVE: Packing up one of my many antique wicker picnic baskets.
OPPOSITE: After a visit to the local farmer's market, our dog Winnie is ready to sample some homegrown—and baked—goodies.

A Place for Potting

One of the pleasures of spring in Vermont is the many specimens of flowering fruit trees. And one activity that invariably draws me up to our getaway in the midst of "mud season" is being able to force or coax budded branches from these trees into an early bloom.

My cutting room, which does double duty as our laundry room and pantry (disguised behind painted doors and cabinets), is the perfect place since it's quite cool (important for the buds' blossoming) and allows me enough space to spread out my branches while working with them.

Come summer, you'll find me here, making loose and informal wildflower arrangements from our surrounding fields and local farmer's market. A slip of a single sunflower, tied around a napkin with some long grasses (or raffia), can, I've learned, make a simple place setting special.

At Christmastime, I love to use the birch bark and moss that I scour our woods for, and these natural elements, combined into garlands with small white lights, are truly spectacular on the holiday tree we set up outside on our deck—a warm and welcoming vision amidst our snowy exterior.

But whatever the season, the faux-decoupage wallpaper of our Vermont animal wildlife in silhouette is what makes me as happy as my childhood nickname, "June bug," when indulging in one of my favorite pastimes.

ABOVE: *Natural gifts of a fruitful Vermont summer harvest—gorgeous sunflowers in the afternoon sun on our kitchen counter.*
OPPOSITE: *When planning a late-spring party, I'll incorporate some of my downstate plants and flowers with my local garden varieties to create surprising and colorful arrangements and presentations.*

NAUTICAL AMBIANCE

Red rooms! I often love to quote the late and legendary fashion icon Diana Vreeland when it comes to painting a room red, since as she once famously said, "Red is the great clarifier—bright and revealing. I can't imagine becoming bored with red—it would be like becoming bored with the person you love."

Our getaway in Vermont gave me the opportunity to experiment—albeit with a twist (a bright "lipstick red" wouldn't quite work in our barn-sided little den). So, by dropping down the tone of the paint to a darker red, with a few added drops of black and brown, I knew we had captured the look I wanted.

My first big expenditure with Kevin after we married three-plus decades ago was a sofa bed (now with a new mattress), and it's certainly seen its share of sleepovers over the years. The neutral color of beige seems to be a constant presence in much of my surroundings—including on this couch—and to give it a bit more definition and contrast, I added red welting to the arms and cushions, and I also followed that same dictum—beige with a touch of red—on our pair of undersized but comfy club chairs.

A portrait of a severe-looking gentleman from another era in aging and crackled oil paint—discovered at the Woodward Estate auction—hangs above another of my designs, a small secretary that I decided would be more suitable if transformed into a bar for soft drinks and spirits opposite the sofa.

A *bibliothèque* for our never-ending collection of books fits neatly into one wall, and an unused closet was morphed into a television nook. Underfoot, durable toffee-colored wall-to-wall carpeting unites the elements in this small room.

It's a place for all seasons, but it really turns into our sanctuary when mud season descends upon our beloved land, as it does each spring—a time to hunker down with good books and, particularly for Kevin and me, to catch up on all those marvelous black-and-white films from the '40s and '50s!

ABOVE: *An undersized secretary serves many uses.* **OPPOSITE:** *A corner of our den, with another* bibliothèque *of my design, is a great place to display boats, maps, and sailing prints—all a nod to Kevin's childhood sailing experiences in Marblehead, Massachusetts.*

PART II
CASUAL COMFORTS

RUSTIC ROMANCE

A purist's approach to our mid-century-modern getaway would most likely dictate a more austere decorating scheme, but knowing my family (and friends) the way I do, I felt that a more relaxed and pampered direction would be best—especially in each of our bedrooms—after a hard day of skiing or hiking.

And so with these aspirations in mind, I transformed our master bedroom, with its enchanting views of the Taconic and Green mountains, into a cozy retreat—evoking memorable stays at inns across the country. As Albert Hadley, the well-known and influential interior designer, noted about a bedroom he once designed, "This room could be anywhere—in the country or in town—but it does open on the terrace—making one immediately aware of the setting." And with our mountain and meadow views, Albert's sentiment is very apropros to our own bedroom.

A pale taupe was chosen as a soothing backdrop on the walls surrounding our four-poster cherry wood bed and bench, a pair of comfortable armchairs and matching ottomans are covered in a plush chenille, with the curtains and bed linens in a pink and cream floral pattern, and, except for a small antique toile-covered desk chair, all of the furnishings and fabrics here—like so many other rooms in our homes—are of my design, which allows me the true luxury of testing them out on family, friends, and pets before they ever reach the stores, creating, in effect, my own "laboratory of design."

Black-and-white photographs of one of my favorite cities, Venice, are simply framed and were taken by a good friend, the late graphic designer, Alex Gottfried, based on a dream he had of that same place. A graphic counterpoint to the room's soft ambiance, these images are always a source of inspiration to me in my own photographic work.

In keeping with that same aesthetic, I decided that our sons' rooms could also capture a sense of a getaway—yet transcend the "perfectly appointed" room—especially when guests stay there. This was definitely a room to have some decorating fun in—without seeming too "cute." The realistic log cabin wallpaper that serves as the backdrop of their room was inspired by a trip that I took with my family to Sante Fe, New Mexico.

PREVIOUS SPREAD: *I completely relax the instant I step into our floral bedroom. I used another circular mirror as I did in our sitting room in Westchester since I love its impact on a room—one of the reasons I enjoy designing furniture so much.*
OPPOSITE: *Our four-poster bed is supposed to be off-limits to our menagerie of dogs, but sometimes Dudley will nap as close as he can to it!*

ABOVE: *The light in our bedroom is early morning and direct—occasionally tempting me to spend a full morning capturing some of my favorite mountain views on canvas or paper.*
OPPOSITE: *I had so much fun designing this secretary, with its secret compartments and drawers here filled with my personal memorabilia, that I knew I would want to wake up to it—and to the memory of its creation—each morning.*

ABOVE: *A small boudoir chair that I found at a nearby secondhand store has a slipcover made of towels, replete with my monogram, for a television segment I did for The Oprah Winfrey Show. One of my early watercolors hangs above.* OPPOSITE: *A close-up of bathroom paraphernalia—old and new— dressed up with some of my collections of glass prisms.*

RIGHT: *My sons' "Telluride Room" in all its Western glory. A realistic-looking log cabin wallpaper gives depth to this small bedroom, while the wooden Venetian blinds add a bit of authenticity and help to filter the strong rays of afternoon sunlight.*

ABOVE: *Birch boxes and books from Kevin's childhood continue the room's "Wild West" ambiance.* OPPOSITE, CLOCKWISE FROM UPPER LEFT: *A built-in set of drawers, painted a deep hunter green, are filled with our sons' ski and fishing garb, often borrowed by me; a wrangler's breakfast, served in our enamelware, which was discovered on a photography jaunt to Montana; extra terry-cloth robes, towels, and buffalo-plaid nightshirts are always at the ready for unexpected guests.*

ABOVE AND OPPOSITE: *I love faux wallpaper and the different moods it can create in a powder room. Here are two examples in our getaway. The* bibliothèque *design by my friend, the late Richard Lowell Neas, makes it a fun "reading room," while the fishing motif is more in keeping with our locale near the Battenkill River.*

PART III
MOUNTAIN SPIRIT

GOLDEN MORNINGS

Over the last thirty-plus years, I've been a regular visitor to Vermont, not just in winter for skiing and autumn for the gorgeous, changing colors but also in the short, but enchanting, summer—with its warm days and cool nights, only interrupted sporadically by spectacular thunder and lightning storms.

My husband, Kevin—a native New Englander—was, I discovered as we began our search for a Vermont getaway, a great fan of screened-in porches, both for their obvious charm and for the protection they offer against the ever-present mosquitoes and notorious black flies of early summer in the Northeast.

I've now been won over by the virtues of this time-tested and venerable New England classic, and our porch is a favorite family destination in the warmer months for a myriad of activities—from leisurely breakfasts to afternoon naps and evening cocktails. Dinners illuminated by a plethora of candles in all shapes and sizes are often accentuated by firefly dances.

And just like on the sleeping porches of the past, there is a corner for when visitors ask—or occasionally beg—to sleep out on a fairly comfortable yet, at the same time, primitive setting.

A simple Adirondack-style bed is arranged on an angle in one corner, with inexpensive mosquito netting hooked from the ceiling in a graceful drape, while a makeshift table of two-by-fours is covered with an antique linen tablecloth.

In keeping with the rusticity of the setting, we have, for our adventurous visitors, simple elements for their morning ablutions, such as a natural sponge and an enamelware bucket, a tray with a collection of soaps, and, of course, one of my favorites—for its functionality and old-fashioned style—an oscillating table fan.

A touch of the '60s, my canvas butterfly chair not only fits in seamlessly here and folds up easily, but it also suits all shapes and sizes. Clean-lined lamps and a metal tray table with a windup clock—necessary amenities for modern-day comfort—don't detract from the rich views beyond.

PREVIOUS SPREAD: *One of our favorite—and our guests' favorite—views from our back deck. To the left, the Taconics, and to the right, the Green Mountains, all anchored by the valley between, and able to be enjoyed from morning to night from our wooden Adirondack chairs— to my eyes, better than any front-row seat in a movie theater and nature's glory at its best.* OPPOSITE: *A stunningly simple vignette—easy to duplicate with some mosquito netting, a vintage bed, and bits and pieces found at flea markets . . . and in attics.*

ABOVE: *All the basics for a wake-up on our porch.*
OPPOSITE: *To greet these views in the morning, I must admit, is an enchanting paean to Vermont.*

NATURAL GARDEN EMBELLISHMENTS

Being an avid gardener at a vacation home is a luxury, but, at the same time, presents some interesting challenges.

I often think with admiration of the hardy stock of farmers who worked this difficult land, with its short growing season, and I knew as a weekend resident that I also had to make some realistic choices.

Planting a vegetable garden was unfortunately not an option since being able to attend to the necessities of tasks, such as tying up tomato and bean vines and keeping small, pesky creatures off the basil and lettuce, would create obstacles that even the most talented gardener without the luxury of daily maintenance would balk at.

I decided to limit myself to tending to what was indigenous to the land when we moved in: lovely lilac bushes and trees, scented apple blossoms and their fruit, some hardy hydrangeas, and wildflowers.

We are blessed in this part of Vermont to have a thriving farmer's market where local farmers showcase and sell their produce, from luscious hybrid tomatoes in a rainbow of colors, to vibrant sunflowers the size of our next-door neighbor's cow's face. A stroll through our local farmer's market is, for me, like a trip through Alice's Wonderland.

I also realized, alas, that my cabbage roses probably wouldn't feel comfortable here, so I happily contented myself with the branches of winterberry that I gather during fall, winter, and spring.

ABOVE: *A prized find at our local antiques fair held each summer, this unusual and comfortable wooden bench needed just a sanding and a few coats of paint; it now sits next to a stone toadstool found at our local nursery.* **OPPOSITE:** *An antique urn, a tomato plant, and some berries create a winning combination, as seen on our screened-in porch overlooking the garden bench.*

PASTORAL VIGNETTES

anciful or informal, my memories of entertaining in the countryside are always pleasurable. Whether recapturing festive meals through our photography albums, nostalgic scrapbooks, or just in my mind's eye, I thoroughly enjoy the coming together of good food and drink, fun table settings, and, of course, great friends.

One of the key ingredients for me is a simple meal with local produce as the star attraction, but I also use another element for my inspiration—textiles. And being a collector of new and old ones—gathered from trips as far away as Istanbul's Grand Bazaar and Paris's Clignancourt flea market to as close as our local summer antique fairs held nearby at the polo grounds of the historic Hildene house in Manchester—I often find that something as simple as the color found in a great piece of fabric, such as a tomato-red scarf or a plaid shawl, can be the inspiration for a dish that will make its

appearance on that evening's menu.

Effortless entertaining means bringing out a mixture of old and new tableware and utensils. I dust off my enamelware and Fiestaware and, combined with my collection of local Bennington pottery and a mélange of flatware, Bakelite, and silverware, these elements all magically combine to create a whimsical setting.

And by effortless, I really mean planning and organizing well ahead—the best way, I've found, to put my guests (and myself) at ease.

So with a choice of several romantic and atmospheric locales in our getaway to dine—our wraparound deck (great for an al fresco breakfast), screened-in porch (perfect for dinner), and surrounding fields and grass-banked streams (divine for picnics)—Kevin and I will often indulge our guests—and ourselves—in impromptu and moveable feasts, depending on the time of day and our ever-changing Vermont weather.

ABOVE: *Preparations for a late-autumn lunch.* OPPOSITE: *A favorite shawl from India decorates our collapsible and portable wicker table, a bucolic setting for breakfast on the deck outside our bedroom's glass sliding doors.*

RIGHT: *By hanging an old chandelier overhead, our disparate mixture of outdoor furniture is elevated to a true gathering spot for late afternoon and evening dining.*
FOLLOWING SPREAD: *A walk in the woods during an autumn day with one of my three dogs, Lola.*

RESOURCES

PURCHASE

A. I. Friedman
Frames, paper, art supplies, journals
Port Chester, NY 10573
1-914-937-7351
www.aifriedman.com

Alva Upholstery
Upholstery, window treatments
Port Chester, NY 10573
1-914-935-0776

Anthropologie
Tabletop, decorative accessories
Trenton, SC 29847
1-800-309-2500
www.anthropologie.com

Apple Computers
Personal computer
1-800-676-2775
www.apple.com

Arcade Book Sellers, Inc.
Decorative books
Rye, NY 10580
1-914-967-0966

Archivia Bookstore
Decorative books
New York, NY 10021
1-212-570-9565
www.archiviabooks.com

Bamboula
Decorative accessories
St. John, U.S. Virgin Islands
00830-6104
1-340-693-8699
www.bamboulastjohn.com

Barclay Butera
Furniture
1-212-207-8665
www.barclaybuterahome.com

Bassett Furniture Industries
Furniture, decorative accessories
1-877-525-7070
www.bassettfurniture.com

Brunschwig & Fils, Inc.
Fabrics, wallpaper
1-914-684-5800
www.brunschwig.com

Calico Corners
Fabrics
Kennett Square, PA 19348
1-800-213-6366
www.calicocorners.com

Carleton V, Ltd.
Fabrics
New York, NY 10022
1-718-706-7780
www.carletonvltd.com

Carpet Trends, Inc.
Carpeting, area rugs
Rye, NY 10580
1-914-967-5188
www.carpettrends.com

Chatsworth
Vintage furniture, tabletop
Mamaroneck, NY 10543
1-914-698-1001
www.chatsworthauction.com

Chelsea House
Decorative accessories
Gastonia, NC 28053
1-704-867-5926
www.chelseahouseinc.com

Cindy Rinfret
*Lighting, tabletop, antiques, furniture,
decorative accessories*
Rinfret, Ltd.
Greenwich, CT 06830
1-203-622-0000
www.rinfretltd.com

Classic Upholstery
Upholstery, window treatments
Norwalk, CT 06851
1-203-845-8776

Colleen Mullaney
Stylist
www.colleenmullaney.com

Corner Bookstore
Decorative books
New York, NY 10128
1-212-831-3554

Crate & Barrel
Lighting, tabletop, furniture
Northbrook, IL 60062
1-800-967-6696
www.crateandbarrel.com

Decorative Interiors, Inc
Decorative pillows, furniture
Manchester Center, VT 05255
1-802-362-3574
www.decorativeinteriors.com

Depot 62
Antique furniture, rugs, lighting, tabletop
Manchester, VT 05254
1-802-366-8229

Floral Fashions
Flowers, floral arrangements
Port Chester, NY 10573
1-914-937-83871
www.floralfashionsonline.com

Frontgate
Outdoor furniture
West Chester, OH 45069
1-888-263-9850
www.frontgate.com

Ginny's Paper Linen
Custom hand towels
1-914-498-4250
www.ginnyspaperlinen.com

Gregory Sahagian & Son Inc.
Awnings
Hartsdale, NY 10530
1-914-949-9877
www.gssawning.com

Hemming Birds
Window treatments
Bedford Hills, NY 10507
1-914-666-5812

Hiden Galleries
Antiques
Stamford, CT 06902
1-203-363-0003
www.hidengalleries.net

Hoagland's of Greenwich
Tabletop, candles
Greenwich, CT 06830
1-888-640-9577
www.hoaglands.com

Homegoods
1-800-614-4663
www.homegoods.com

Ikea
1-800-434-4532
www.ikea-usa.com

The Isabel O'Neil Studio
Decorative painted objects
New York, NY 10128
1-212-348-4464
www.isabeloneil.org

Indigo Seas
Decorative objects, books, antiques, tabletop, furniture
Los Angeles, CA 90048
1-310-550-8758

Jean Simmers, Ltd.
Interior Design
Rye, NY 10580
1-914-967-8533

JCPenney
Furniture, bedding, rugs, lighting, tabletop
Plano, TX 75024
1-800-322-1189
www.jcp.com

Kaas Glassworks
Decoupage plates
New York, NY 10014
1-212-366-0322
www.kaasglassworks.com

The Kellogg Collection, Inc.
Furniture, decorative accessories
Washington, DC 20016
www.kelloggcollection.com

Kids Supply Co.
Decorative pillows
New York, NY 10128
1-212-426-1200
www.kidssupply.com

Lillian August
Decorative objects, furniture
Norwalk, CT 06851
1-203-847-1596
www.lillianaugust.com

Le Beastro
Dog grooming
Rye, NY 10580
1-914-921-0279

The Museum of American Folk Art
Decorative accessories
New York, NY 10019
1-212-265-1040
www.folkartmuseum.com

Neiman Marcus
Decorative objects
New York, NY 10018
1-888-888-4757
www.neimanmarcus.com

Poplar Woods
Cabinetry, architectural design, woodwork
Jerry Larsen
Norwalk, CT 06854
1-203-846-8785

Pottery Barn
Tabletop
1-888-779-5176
www.potterybarn.com

Ralph Lauren
Lighting, furniture, bedding,
decorative accessories
New York, NY 10022
1-888-475-7674
www.ralphlauren.com

Restoration Hardware
Lighting, furniture, bedding,
decorative accessories
Corte Madera, CA 94925
1-800-910-9845
www.restorationhardware.com

Rye Camera
Rye, NY 10580
1-914-967-2164
www.ryecamera.com

Rye Ridge Tile
Tile flooring
Port Chester, NY 10573
1-914-939-1100
www.ryeridgetile.com

Saint Ouen Porte de
Clignancourt Flea Market
Decorative accessories
Paris, France
33 (0) 8 92 70 57 65
www.marchesauxpuces.fr

Shoreline Pools
Stamford, CT 06902
1-203-357-1544
www.shorelinepools.com

Simon Pearce Glass
Glassware, tabletop
Windsor, VT 05089
1-802-674-6280
www.simonpearce.com

Smith & Noble
Window shades
Corona, CA 92881
1-909-734-4444
www.smithandnoble.com

Studio Cabán
Entryway decoupage
Angela Cabán
Brooklyn, NY 11231
1-646-229-1252
www.studiocabán.com

Tiffany & Company
Silver, picture frames
New York, NY 10022
1-800-843-3269
www.tiffany.com

Toni Gallagher Interiors
Interior design
Rye, NY 10580
1-914-967-3594
www.tonigallagherinteriors.com

Treillage, Ltd.
Decorative pillows, furniture
New York, NY 10021
1-212-988-8800
www.treillageonline.com

Your Gardening Angel
Landscaping
Stamford, CT 06902
1-203-531-1837

Waterford
Glassware
1-866-714-0592
www.waterford.com

Wisteria
Decorative accessories, accent furniture
Carrollton, TX 75006
1-800-320-9757
www.wisteria.com

Yves Delorme
Bedding
Charlottesville, VA 22902
1-800-322-3911
www.yvesdelorme.com

VERMONT

Agnes Rethy
Freelance stylist
Westport, CT 06880
1-203-216-3057

Beacon Hill
Decorative fabrics, furniture
Foxboro, MA 02035
1-800-333-3777
www.beaconhilldesign.com

Blind Buck Interiors
Slipcovers, upholstery, window
treatments
Salem, NY 12865
1-518-854-9361

Comollo Antiques
Decorative accessories
Manchester Center, VT 05255
1-802-362-7188
www.comollo.com

Esther Sheldon
Curtains
Pawlet, VT 05761
1-802-325-3376

F. Schumacher & Co.
Wall coverings, fabrics
New York, NY 10016
1-800-523-1200
www.fschumacher.com

Initial Ideas
Embroidery, engraving
Rutland, VT 05701
www.initialideasinc.com

L.L. Bean
*Decorative accessories, pillows,
tabletop*
Freeport, ME 04033
1-800-441-5713
www.llbean.com

Lucinda O'Connell
Painting instructor
St. Thomas, USVI
1-340-514-2432
www.artbylucinda.com

Mary Farrell
Wallpapering
1-914-948-4962
www.homesidebuilding.com

Mottahedeh, Inc.
Tabletop
Cranbury, NJ 08512
1-800-242-3050
www.mottahedeh.com

Mettowee Mill Nursery
Landscaping, gardens
Dorset, VT 05251
1-802-325-3007
www.mettoweemillnursery.com

Miller Earth Designs
Landscaping, gardens
Liz Miller
Manchester Center, VT 05255
1-802-375-2698
www.millerearthdesigns.com

Nantucket Antique Society
Decorative objects
Nantucket, MA 02554
1-508-228-1894
www.nha.org

Nicole Keane
Interior design
Rowayton, CT 06853
1-203-222-7714

Northshire Bookstore
Decorative books
Manchester Center, VT 05255
1-802-362-2200
www.northshirebookstore.com

Orvis
Fishing equipment, home décor
1-888-235-9763
www.orvis.com

R. K. Miles Hardware
Kitchen design, bathroom design
Abby Morgan
Manchester, VT 05254
1-802-362-1952
www.rkmiles.com

Robert Niles Contracting
Wallpapering
North Bennington, VT 05257
1-802-688-6882

Seabrook Wallcoverings, Inc.
Wallpaper
Memphis, TN 38122
1-800-238-9152
www.seabrookwallpaper.com

Sid Badger
Painting
1-802-645-0450
serendipityhomestaging@live.com

Tom Molloy
Contractor
Manchester, VT 05254

Union Village, Ltd.
Adirondack chairs
Greenwich, NY 12834
1-518-692-2034
www.unionvillageltd.com

ABOVE: *Ready for breakfast.*
PHOTO ON PAGE 207: *An early springtime nest as seen from my bedroom window.*

ACKNOWLEDGMENTS

To create a book is always a team effort and my team is extraordinary. Starting off with gratitude to Sarah Palomba, who gracefully and brilliantly spearheaded this project with the assistance of Phil Pineau and Nick Madden. Larry Kirshbaum, a true gentleman and my agent, was invaluable. At Rizzoli, my editor Kathleen Jayes, along with Claire Gierczak, Anthony Petrillose, Jessica Napp, and Colin Hough-Trapp, under the leadership of the publisher Charles Miers, worked with us through this book's exciting process. Thanks to Doug Turshen and David Huang for their design guidance.

This book could not have been produced without the keen eyes and talent of my wonderful team of photographers Nancy Elizabeth Hill, Phillip Ennis, Pedro Garcia, Trel Brock, Fran Janik, Bob Capazzo, Michel Arnaud, Keith Scott Morton, Charles Maraia, Leo Sorel, Quentin Bacon, Jennifer Levy, and Keller + Keller. Joanne Seipel of Floral Fashions helped me create the interior floral magic, while Mike Murphy and his crew cultivated our New York gardens—whatever the season. Thanks also to our friends at Mettowee Nursery and Liz Miller in Vermont for their creative landscaping.

Kim Kimball discovered our Vermont getaway, while Stephanie Fischer Zernin led us to our carriage house formerly owned by the gracious Pat and Frank Noonan. John Halpin, Tom Molloy and Adam Kapelanski flawlessly executed my design vision. Thanks to Lucinda O'Connell, Matt Johnson, Sherri McAdams, Rob Spilman, Joyce Brown and, of course, FIT, for opening my eyes to the world of design. My talented colleagues at JCPenney beginning with Charlie Chinni, Allen Questrom, Mike Ullman, Peter McGrath, Ken Hicks, John Kendig, Jeff Allison, Rick Jones, and Deb Evans—all pros in the world of retail.

Gratitude to Lynn von Kersting and Cindy Rinfret whose shops never cease to inspire me, and to Cathy Burke, Colleen Mullaney, Agnes Rethy, and Jeffrey Bilhuber—who have the designer's eye beyond compare. Special thanks to Carolyn Schultz and Barbara Marks. One can't get through life without girlfriends—my sisters Jeanne and Mary, and the fantastic Toni, Gwen, Nancy, Kathy, Bridget, Liz, and Sue, all of whom always sustained me through this journey. And of course my five brothers, Tom, John, Jim, Justin, and Paul.

For nurturing my body and soul—Tony Hoyt, Steve Tyrell, Rye Country Store, The Barrows House, Le Mistral, June & Ho, Deux Amis, Marilu Tedesco, Jane Farhi, Drew DeMann, Jaclyn Knight, Susan Wheeler and her Equinox team, and Ritz Carlton Destination Club.

And what would this book be without Dudley, Lola, and Winnie, my beloved four-footed friends!

PHOTOGRAPHY CREDITS

PURCHASE PHOTO CREDITS
All photographs by Nancy Elizabeth Hill except
the following:

P 6 Michel Arnaud (top left); Chris Madden (bottom left)
P 10 © Jennifer Levy
P 13 Chris Madden
P 17 Bob Capazzo
PP 18–19 all images Chris Madden, except bottom left and
   bottom right, Nancy Elizabeth Hill
P 22 © Keith Scott Morton
P 33 Charles Maraia
PP 34–35 Phillip Ennis
PP 36–37, 39 (top left) © Trel Brock
P 39 Phillip Ennis (bottom right)
P 48 Chris Madden
P 49 Leo Sorel
P 50 Charles Maraia
PP 52–53, 54, 58, 60–61, 64–65 (top left) © Trel Brock
P 66, 67 (bottom right and bottom left) Quentin Bacon
P 77 Chris Madden (top right)
PP 78–79 Bob Capazzo
P 80 Chris Madden
P 81 Charles Maraia
P 84 Phillip Ennis
P 86–87 © Trel Brock
PP 102–103 © Keith Scott Morton
P 104 Chris Madden
P 105 © Trel Brock
PP 112–113 © Jennifer Levy
P 117 Quentin Bacon
PP 118, 120–121 © Trel Brock

P 122 Phillip Ennis
P 123 Quentin Bacon
P 126 Chris Madden
P 127 Michel Arnaud
P 130 Chris Madden
P 131 Bob Capazzo (top left, top right, and bottom right)
PP 132–133 Chris Madden
P 137 Phillip Ennis (top left); © Keith Scott Morton
   (bottom right); Bob Capazzo (bottom left)
PP 138–139 © Keith Scott Morton
P 140, 142–143, 146–147 Chris Madden

VERMONT PHOTO CREDITS
All photographs by Nancy Elizabeth Hill except
the following:

P 148 Keller + Keller
P 150 © Fran Janik
P 151 Chris Madden
PP 152–153, 154 © Fran Janik
PP 155, 156–157, 159, 160, 162–163, 168 © Trel Brock
P 169 Keller + Keller
P 170 Chris Madden
PP 172–173, 177, 184, 185 (top left and bottom right),
   186 © Trel Brock
PPP 188–189 © Fran Janik
PP 194–195 Chris Madden
P 196 © Fran Janik
PP 198–199 © Trel Brock
PP 200–201 © Fran Janik
p 205 Phillip Ennis
Additional photo retouching by Pedro S. Garcia

First published in the United States of America in 2010
by Rizzoli International Publications, Inc.
300 Park Avenue South
New York, NY 10010
www.rizzoliusa.com

© 2009 Chris Casson Madden

2010 2011 2012 2013 / 10 9 8 7 6 5 4 3 2 1

Distributed in the U.S. trade by Random House, New York

Printed in China

ISBN: 978-0-8478-3370-2

Library of Congress Cataloging-in-Publication Data:
2010927315

Art Direction: Doug Turshen with David Huang